LESLIE LINSLEY

First Steps
In Quilting

LESLIE LINSLEY

First Steps

In Quilting

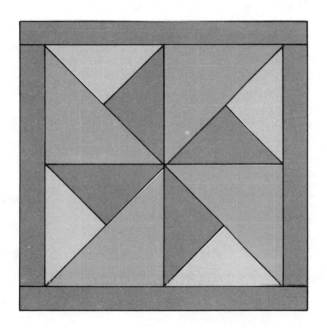

Doubleday & Company, Inc., Garden City, New York

CONTENTS

Book Three

FIRST STEPS IN QUILTING FOR THE HOLIDAY SEASON   *1*

Acknowledgments

I'd like to thank Robby Smith for her contributions to the design and production of the projects. I am also grateful to Kate Rumsey and Janet O'Hara for their crafting expertise.

My appreciation is extended to V.I.P. fabrics, Laura Ashley fabrics, and Fairfield Processing Corporation for their generous contributions to this project.

INTRODUCTION

Today the whole country is quilt-conscious, but quilt making has been part of America's way of life since our country was first settled. Patchworks and appliqués were initially made out of necessity. Thrifty North American settlers pieced together scraps of fabric from worn-out clothing to make things to keep warm. Later, making patchworks became a social event, a means of socializing while being productive during cold winter nights. The history of our American way of life was stitched into those early quilts at quilting bees where patterns and gossip were exchanged.

Only one form of needlework is our own American folk art and that is our pieced patchwork, the sewing together of fabrics to create a pieced whole cloth. To the women who made our earliest quilts, every scrap of fabric took on a new importance. They began to look at the pieces with an eye to seeing what simple shapes could be created from them. American women developed pieced and appliquéd patterns that are still cherished, copied, revised, reproduced, and faithfully restored today.

If you are new to quilting, perhaps it is best to know from the start how easy it is. One can't help but say, "I could do that!" when first confronted with a quilting project. It is the simplest form of sewing, mostly involving straight line stitches on the machine or by hand. Once you learn the basic techniques for making patchwork, appliqué, and quilting patterns, the variety of projects you can make is endless. Unlike the early quilters, today's needleworker has a wide assortment of fabrics to choose from. There are also quilting aids for every possible situation. For example, there are self-adhesive templates you can buy for most of the popular quilting designs. You simply stick the design in place, quilt around the shape, and then remove the template. You are left with a perfectly quilted outline. You can also find almost any popular quilt pattern, packaged with the yardage of fabric figured for any size bed and complete directions for making the quilt. There are cutting tools that make it a snap to cut all the pieces for a patchwork quilt. One that I am especially fond of is a roller that looks like a pizza cutter. You line up your fabric and roll the cutter along your marked lines. There are plastic grid sheets for enlarging or decreasing designs, plastic templates, star makers which aid in making an 8-point star, and special rulers marked with cutting lines, angles, and different seam allowances. These are but a few of the many products available especially for quilting. So you see, there isn't any reason why even a complete novice can't learn to be an expert quilter.

Since this book is a first-steps primer, we will start off with very simple projects that you can finish quickly. Instant gratification is, after all, what spurs us on to more rewarding challenges. You will learn how to quilt almost any fabric and what to do with it. You will learn to make some interesting household and personal accessories. It's fun to decorate with quilted projects, which always lend an air of warmth and comfort to almost any room. Once you've learned how to do patchwork and appliqué on a place mat or a baby's bib, you'll be inspired to take on a larger project such as a quilt or wall hanging. The process is all the same, the dimensions are the only changes. So don't be intimidated by that gorgeous antique quilt you saw on your friend's bed or hanging in the fancy boutique. If you can hold a needle and thread, you can quilt.

Quilting terms

Appliqué:

The technique of creating a design by cutting a shape from one fabric and stitching it to a contrasting fabric background.

Backing:

The bottom piece of fabric that is of the same weight as the top. This piece can be a solid or a printed fabric that matches the design on the top. Muslin is a good, inexpensive fabric often used for backing a quilted project.

Basting:

Securing the top, batting, and backing together with long loose stitches before quilting. These stitches are removed after each section is quilted.

Batting:

The soft lining that makes a quilted fabric puffy and gives a quilt warmth. Batting comes in a variety of thicknesses, each appropriate for different kinds of projects.

Binding:

The way the raw edges of fabric are finished. One binding technique is to cut the backing slightly larger than the top piece. After you've stitched the top, batting, and backing together, this overlap is brought forward, turned, and hemmed to the top, creating a finished border. Contrasting fabric or bias binding can also be used to finish the edges of a fabric.

Block:

Sometimes referred to as a square. Geometric or symmetrical pieces of fabric are sewn together to create a design. Finished blocks are sewn together, usually with a border (or sash) between each square.

Patchwork:

Sewing together of fabric pieces to create an entire design. Sometimes the shapes form a geometric block. The blocks are then sewn together to make up the completed project.

Piecing:

Joining patchwork pieces together to form a design on the block.

Quilting:

Stitching together 2 layers of fabric with a layer of batting between.

Quilting patterns:

The lines or markings on the fabric that make up the design. Small hand or machine stitches quilt along these lines, which might be straight or curved or made up of elaborate curlicued patterns.

Sash or strips:

The narrow pieces of fabric used to frame the individual blocks and join them together. These are often of a contrasting color.

Setting:

Joining the quilt blocks to form the finished top piece of a quilt.

Template:

A pattern that is rigid and full size. It can be cut from cardboard or plastic acetate. Some quilters prefer sandpaper templates because they are of the acceptable weight and won't slide on the fabric. The template is used to trace the design elements. When cutting the fabric, you will usually add 1/4-inch seam allowance. However, all templates provided here will include the seam allowance for easy and accurate cutting.

Top:

The top of a quilting project is the front layer of fabric with the right side showing.

Materials for quilting

Fabric:

Fabric is the main concern of the quilting process. Traditionally, of course, quilt makers didn't buy fabric especially for quilts, but rather used what was on hand. In this way a quilted project became a family "documentary" with bits and pieces of worn-out or outgrown clothing cut up and pieced together.

Today we have so many different kinds of fabric, patterns, and colors available that it is often more difficult and yet more exciting to plan a project. Small projects enable you to use up the scraps you may already have on hand.

Cotton has always been the favorite fabric for quilting projects, as well as cotton blends such as polyester which is drip-dry and won't shrink. These are most readily available in every print and color imaginable. For the best results when combining fabrics in one project, choose those with the same fiber content.

If you are making a large project with various cottons, it is always recommended that you wash the fabric first to preshrink it.

I have used many calico prints for my projects. These are small, overall designs that come in a multitude of colors and patterns that work together. Though they are of a country style, they seem to work well on any object and seem traditional and contemporary at the same time. Laura Ashley cotton prints are also used and recommended as good fabrics for quilting. The prints and colors make any project seem elegant.

Old sheets that have been softened with wear are excellent for backing material. And all the pretty printed sheets made today are equally wonderful for quilting. Since the fabric is already cut to size for any bed you don't have to piece it as you would with fabric that is 36 or 45 inches wide.

Needles:

These are often called "betweens." The sizes most commonly used for quilting are #7 and #8 sharps. An embroidery needle in the same size is also good. It is especially useful for appliqué and piecing.

Thread:

Match the thread to the color of the fabric. Cotton-blend thread is best for appliqué and piecing. There is a special quilting thread that has a coating to make it stronger, though I sometimes use regular thread for running

stitches to quilt a fabric. Other times embroidery floss is perfect, especially when quilting with embroidery stitches. The floss comes in every shade of every color you could possibly need to match your fabric.

Scissors:

If you invest in good-quality scissors from the start, they will be the best investment you'll ever make. This is especially true if you plan to do a lot of quilting. A good pair of scissors can cut a straight line of fabric without fraying or pulling it. Do not use them for anything but cutting fabric. If you cut paper with your fabric scissors, they will never perform as well again.

It's always a good idea to have small snipping scissors handy. These will be invaluable, especially for hand stitching.

Thimble:

Not an absolute must, but a definite plus if you can get used to wearing it. If you are making a project with hand-sewn stitching, you will be taking 3 to 6 stitches at a time through 2 layers of fabric and a layer of batting. A thimble will make the work easier, quicker, and less painful.

Templates:

Cardboard, such as shirt board or oaktag, is perfect for cutting templates. Clear plastic is also used (sold in sheets in art supply stores and precut shapes through craft shops). (See page xxxi for sources.) Plastic is preferred because it keeps a clean, crisp edge and you can see through it, giving you an idea of how a piece will look before you cut it out.

Markers:

A soft pencil is good for tracing and transferring designs to the fabric. There are pens with water-soluble ink for this purpose as well. You can mark on the fabric and, when the quilting is finished, any marks that show can be easily removed without scrubbing by simply using a plant mister. Chalk is often used to mark dark material. A tracing wheel and dressmaker's carbon paper is another method for transferring designs to fabric in order to quilt. These are available in most notion departments.

Iron:

It is impossible to do any sewing project without an iron at your elbow. Use a steam iron for quick and easy piecing. A lightweight iron is a must and some sewing experts keep a well-padded stool next to them for quick ironing of seams between stitching.

Frame and hoop:

Most quilting can be done on a large hoop. For many, a full-size quilting frame is essential when making any size quilt. The size of the hoop depends on the project. You can find these through quilting stores or mail-order sources.

Rulers:

A yardstick and ruler are necessary. A metal ruler can be used as a straightedge when cutting templates and, because it is thin, will lie flat on the fabric and give you the most accurate measure. A yardstick is helpful for cutting lengths of fabric where you must mark and cut at least 36 inches at one time.

Quilting basics

Estimating amount of fabric:

Quilting tends to draw up the fabric slightly so that the size of the finished work is reduced a bit. While I've figured all the measurements to the 1/4 inch for all projects in the book, I still recommend cutting border pieces and backing material last to be sure the size of the top hasn't changed. When a project is comprised of many pieces, it's very easy to stitch together two pieces that are slightly "off," but these fractions of an inch can entirely change the dimension of the finished project.

Most fabric is 45 inches wide and I have stated that this width fabric is necessary for certain projects. When it isn't stated, it means that the width is unimportant to the amount given.

When estimating yardage for a bed quilt, measure your bed fully made. This means with bed pad, sheets, and blankets over the mattress. Measure the length, width, and depth including the box spring. Decide if you want a slight overhang, an overhang with a dust ruffle, or a drop to the floor, and whether or not the quilt will extend up and over the pillows.

To figure exact yardage, make a diagram on grid paper. One grid block represents 4 inches or 6 inches, depending on how large the finished project will be. Use this diagram as a guide when sewing together pieces for the final project. If a quilt or wall hanging isn't the exact size for your use, it can often be changed by adding to, or subtracting from, the border measurements. This will not change the design and might even improve the look of the project.

Backing:

The backing is the bottom layer of any quilted fabric and is usually made from a lightweight fabric such as cotton. Unbleached muslin is an especially good material to use for quilts because it is available 60 inches wide and is quite inexpensive. Sometimes the backing may show as a border, for example. In this case, you might want to select a color that matches or contrasts nicely with the colors used on the top fabric.

When you have determined how much fabric you'll need for the backing, you may find that you'll have to piece panels together to obtain the correct size to match the finished dimensions of the project. This may be true with a quilt, wall hanging, or tablecloth, for example. It is best to avoid running a seam down the center of the backing. Instead, cut 3 panels of fabric, and join 2 matching panels to each long side edge of a center panel. Press seams open.

Filler:

The filler for a quilted fabric is usually called quilt batting or fiber fill and is a layer of fibers used between the top fabric and backing. Though it is lightweight and airy, it gives the quilted fabric bulk and warmth. You can buy this by the yard in most fabric stores, five-and-tens, and notion stores. It comes in various thicknesses for different uses. Often I will list thin quilt batting as the preferable material for a specific project. Most batting sold in packages will state what the thickness is best used for, such as a quilted jacket or warm bed quilt. In this way you can buy the best batting for the project. Most batting is of medium thickness and works well for most projects. Therefore the choice of thickness isn't an area of real concern unless specifically stated. When in doubt ask the salesperson who is usually knowledgeable about the materials.

When quilting is done, the batting is secured to the back of the top fabric. Sometimes the quilting is done right through the backing material as well. The quilting threads are stitched through the 2 or 3 layers of material to achieve the three-dimensional effect of quilting.

Enlarging designs:

Almost every design for quilting and pattern pieces in this book is shown full size. However, sometimes a pattern piece is larger than the book page and must be enlarged. In this case the designs are shown on a grid for easy enlargement.

If each square on the grid equals 1 inch, it means you will transfer or copy the design onto graph paper marked with 1-inch squares. Pads or sheets of graph paper are available in art and quilting stores. It's also easy to rule off a sheet of paper in 1-inch squares.

Begin by counting the number of squares on the pattern in the book. Number them horizontally and again vertically. Count the same number of squares on your larger graph and number them in the same way. Copy the design onto your grid one square at a time.

Transferring large designs:

Trace the pattern pieces or quilting designs from the book or from your graphed enlargement. Place a piece of dressmaker's tracing (carbon) paper on the right side of fabric (carbon side down) with traced design on top. Go over all pattern lines with a tracing wheel or ballpoint pen to transfer the design. Remove the carbon and tracing.

Making a template:

Transfer the pattern to the template material by first tracing the design. If you're making a cardboard template, place the tracing face down on the cardboard and rub over each traced line. The outline will come off on the cardboard. For a sharper image, place a piece of carbon paper on the cardboard with the tracing on top. Go over each line with a pencil. Remove the tracing and, using sharp scissors, cut out the design outline from the cardboard. If you're using acetate, place it over the tracing to cut out the exact shape. Another method is as follows: Mark a pattern on paper. Glue this to stiff cardboard or plastic and let dry. Cut along traced outline.

Since you'll be working with several different fabrics, you must determine which fabric will be used for each template. Then, figure out the best layout for getting the most pieces from your fabric. For example, place all triangles on the fabric so they form squares. Mark around each template on the fabric. If seam allowance has not been allocated for the template, each piece must be cut 1/4 inch larger all around. Be sure to leave room for this allowance between template markings.

Sometimes, with very sharp scissors, you can cut out several layers of fabric at once. If you're using lights and darks of one pattern, you can place the light fabric over the dark, mark the top cloth only, and cut through both layers at the same time.

Accuracy is most important in cutting, especially for pieced work. Pin carefully and keep your pattern pieces and fabric flat and smooth.

Piecing:

Although it is not faster, it is often easier to sew by hand. One advantage is that you can take your work with you to stitch in odd moments. Also, some complicated designs are easier to do by hand. Since traditionally quilting was done by hand, this is the preferred method by most. However, if you ma-

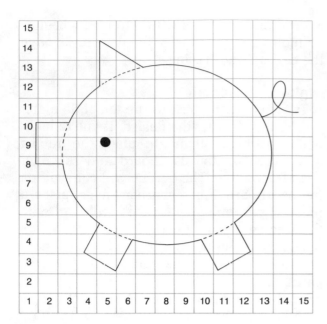

chine-stitch, the work will go faster and be stronger than handwork.

Use a needle of recommended size (see page xi) and sew with small running stitches. Take 8 to 10 stitches per inch. Usually the thread should match the fabric background, but you can also use a contrasting color to emphasize the quilting pattern.

Figs. 1, 2 One easy way of enlarging a design is by numbering the squares on the original pattern and on your larger graph paper. Then transfer each element of the design square by square.

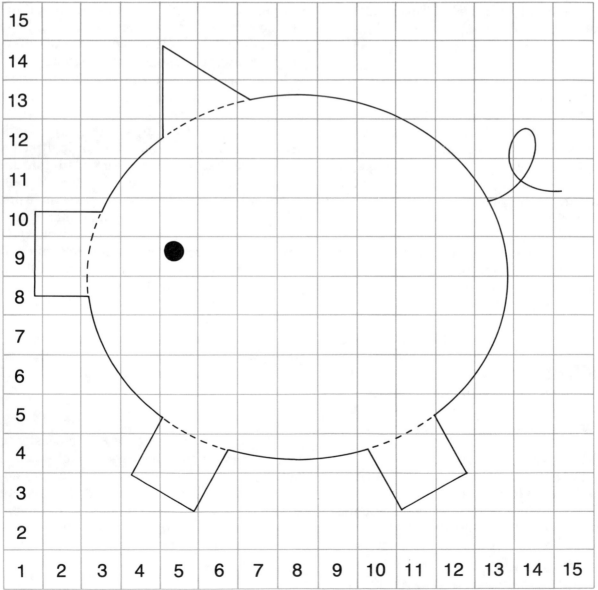

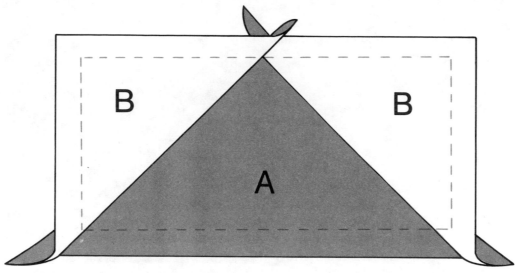

Fig. 3   *Remember not to sew into the seam allowance when joining two pieces that will form a point.*

Sewing points:

Many traditional quilting patterns are created from triangles, diamonds, and similar shapes. The points made by the joining of these shapes present a challenge and require special care.

When stitching 2 pieces together, sew along the stitch line but do not sew into the seam allowance at each point. It helps to mark the finished points with a pin so you can begin and end your seams at these marks.

Sewing curves:

Before turning a curved appliqué piece, stay-stitch along the seam line, then clip or notch evenly spaced cuts along the edge in the seam allowance. Clip all inward curves and notch all outward curves. When the fabric is turned under it will lie flat.

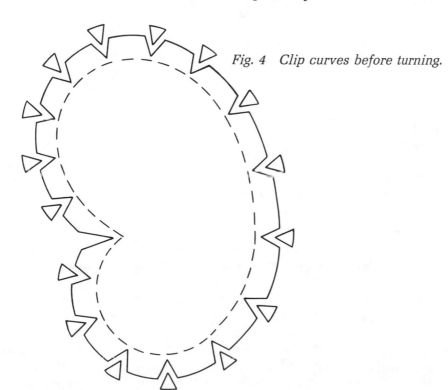

Fig. 4   *Clip curves before turning.*

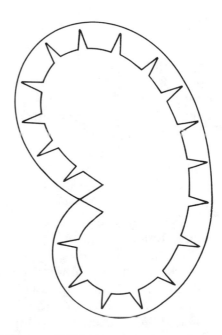

Fig. 5   *Fold edges over template.*

Fig. 6 Clip inside corner to seam.

Inward corner edge:

Place a pin across the point of the stitches and clip up to the stitches in the seam allowance in order to turn the fabric under.

Outward corner edge:

Once you've stitched around a corner, clip off half the seam allowance across the point. Turn fabric back, press seams open and trim excess fabric away.

Turning corners:

It's often a bit difficult to turn corners and continue a seam line. Diagram 1 shows the 3 pieces to be joined. With right sides facing, stitch piece A to piece B as in diagram 2. Next, join C to A as in diagram 3. Leave the needle down in the fabric. Lift the presser foot and clip the seam to the needle. Slide B under C and adjust so the edges of B align with C. Lower the presser foot and stitch along the seam line.

Appliqué:

Using a template, cut out each pattern piece. If there is no seam allowance on your template, add 1/4 inch all around when cutting. All templates here include seam allowance, in which case, once you've cut out the appliqués, trim away the seam allowance on the template. Place the template on the back of the fabric and press all edges over template edges. If the appliqué is curved, clip all edges to seam line before turning.

Pin the appliqué in place on the background fabric and blindstitch or whipstitch it all around. The appliquéd fabric is then backed with batting before you quilt around the design. Use short running stitches around the inside edge of the appliqué.

Fig. 7 Clip off outside corner.

To machine-stitch appliqué, cut the fabric without seam allowance. Edges need not be turned. Pin the fabric in position and zigzag-stitch around the edges. When appliquéing a pointed piece, gradually narrow the zigzag width just before reaching the point on each side.

Sewing circles:

Cut out the fabric and clip evenly around the raw edges in the seam allowance. Turn the edges over the template and press. Position the circular piece on the background

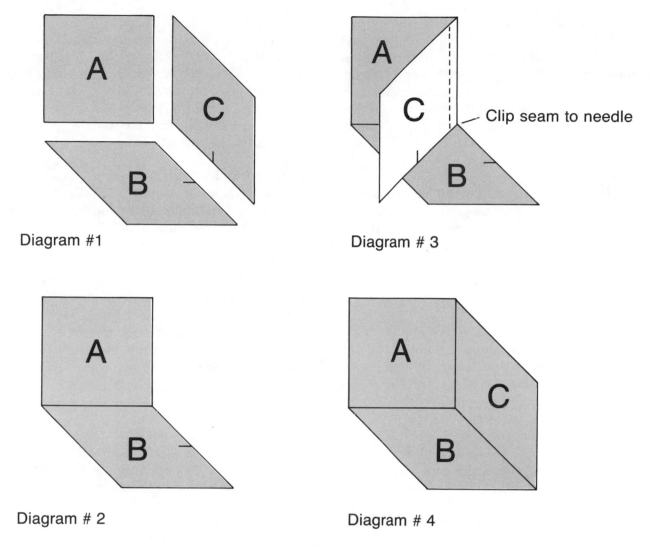

Diagram #1

Diagram # 3

Clip seam to needle

Diagram # 2

Diagram # 4

Fig. 8   Stitch A to B.   Stitch C to A. Clip seam to needle.

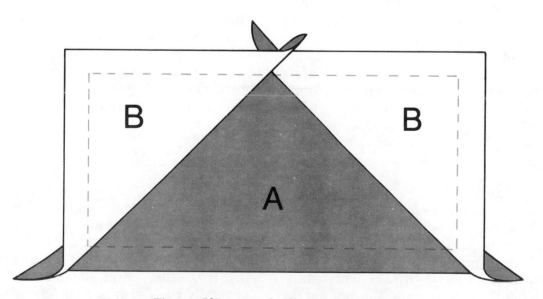

Fig. 9   Clip around edges and turn under.

fabric and stitch together with a blind stitch or whipstitch.

Another method is to machine-stitch around the appliqué piece between the edge and seam lines. This stay stitching makes it easier to turn the seam allowance under. Hand- or machine-stitch to the background fabric.

Joining blocks:

Whether you've appliquéd or pieced a block, the blocks must be joined to make up a quilt, for example. With right sides facing and raw edges aligned, stitch along one edge with a 1/4-inch seam allowance. Continue to make rows of blocks that are then joined.

Borders:

The border around a pillow, quilt, table runner, and the like binds the edges and can be done in one of two ways, depending on how you will finish the corners. Refer to the directions for finishing corners that follow before cutting your strips.

Cut your border strips with several inches added to the length for sewing shrinkage. For the same reason, the width of a strip should also be cut with added seam allowance. The directions for each project are exact and list all pieces to be cut before the sewing steps. In this way you can plan the cutting layout of your fabric to ensure long enough strips for your borders, before cutting the smaller pieces. Consider this when making your quilt and allow for extra inches on the borders.

With right sides facing together, place the front of one raw edge of the top or bottom strip on a quilt edge. Be sure that extra fabric is equal on both ends. Stitch according to directions for the kind of finished corners desired. Repeat on side strips to complete the border.

Finishing corners:

Borders can butt together at the corners or the corners can be mitered. All the border corners for the projects here butt. However, there are many products on the market to ensure perfectly mitered corners. For butting corners, pin the long strips to the sides of the

top with right sides facing. Machine-stitch, leaving a 1/4-inch seam allowance. Repeat with the top and bottom strips. The hem on one edge of the top will be doubled over with the other edge on top of it. If you want to add a square of appliqué to each corner, of a quilt, for example, do so with a matching piece from the overall design.

Joining blocks with a sash:

When you make a quilt or a pillow of quilt blocks, for example, each block is framed with a strip called a sash. Cut each strip the length of a block plus seam allowance. Pin the right side of one sash edge to the right side of one block edge and stitch together. Stitch blocks together to form rows.

Cut long strips for the vertical sashes. Pin right sides of one long edge to raw edge of a row of blocks and stitch together. Join all rows in this way. Be sure to have all seams and blocks lined up perfectly.

Slip stitch edges:

Many of the projects that require turning, and perhaps stuffing, are finished with a slip stitch to close the opening used for turning the fabric right side out. Be sure that the quilt batting does not extend into the seam allowance. Fold each raw edge of the backing and top material to the inside 1/4 inch and slip-stitch together.

Bias binding:

Sometimes a project has a matching or contrasting piece of fabric that runs around the edges to finish them. You can use commercially packaged bias binding which comes in all different colors to match your fabric.

How to quilt

Quilting is the means by which you sew layers of fabric and batting together to produce a padded fabric held together by stitching. It is often warm and decorative and is generally the finishing step in appliqué and

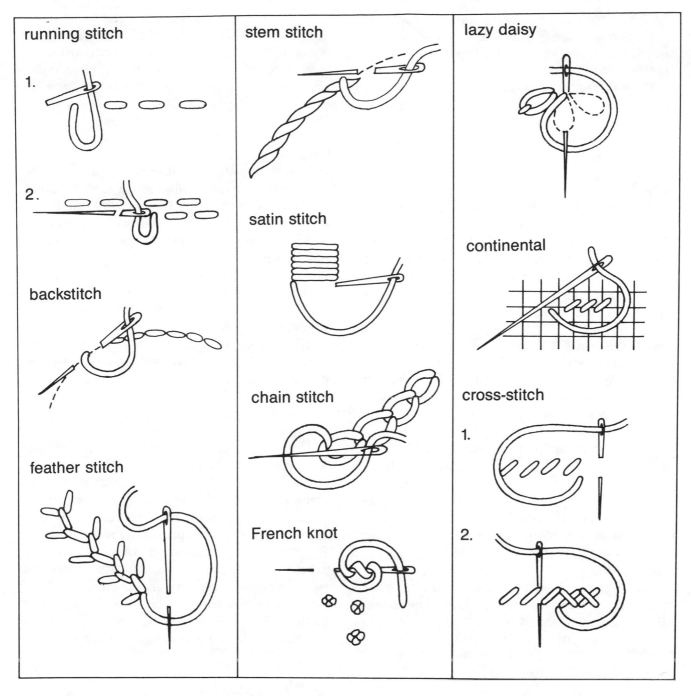

running stitch

1.

2.

backstitch

feather stitch

stem stitch

satin stitch

chain stitch

French knot

lazy daisy

continental

cross-stitch

1.

2.

Fig. 10   Basic Stitches.   These are the stitches you'll find most useful as you quilt.

patchwork projects. You can quilt almost any fabric, making it appear three-dimensional and giving it a sculptured effect. The quilting is what makes a project interesting and gives it a textured look.

Hand quilting:

The most comfortable way to do your quilting is over a frame or in a hoop which keeps the fabric taut, allowing you to make even stitches. It is important to have your fabric and batting basted and marked before quilting each section. When removed from the frame or hoop, your quilting will have a nicely puffed effect.

Give the knotted end a good tug and pull it through the backing fabric into the batting. Keep your thread fairly short and take small running stitches. Follow your premarked quilting pattern.

Machine quilting:

This is easier, quicker, and often preferred for small projects such as bibs, place mats, or Christmas ornaments. It is best to use thin quilt batting for machine stitching. If you set your stitch length for a looser stitch, such as 8–9 stitches per inch, the project will have a hand-stitched look.

Marking patterns:

Before basting the top, batting, and back together, mark the quilting design on the top of the fabric. Spread the top on a hard, flat surface to transfer your design.

A light pencil is one way to mark your pattern. Another is with a water-soluble pen. Once all the quilting is complete, the lines that are visible can be removed with a plant mister. For dark fabrics, use an artist's white grease pencil or chalk. Dressmaker's (carbon) paper and a tracing wheel provide another method for applying the traced design to the fabric.

Use a template when possible to mark your patterns. A yardstick is also handy for marking diagonal lines. Mark on the fabric along both edges of the yardstick, then flip it over and continue to mark along the edge for perfectly spaced quilting lines to follow.

Securing layers:

Place the batting over the wrong side of your backing material and smooth it from the center outward. Place the top fabric, right side up, over the batting and smooth it out. Pin the layers together.

Basting:

Before quilting, you should baste the top fabric, batting, and backing together. To avoid lumps and to hold all fabrics in position, begin at the center of the top piece and baste with long, loose stitches outward, creating a sunburst pattern. There should be about 6 inches between the basted lines at the edge of the fabric. These stitches will be cut away as you do your quilting.

Outlining:

This is the method of quilting just outside the edges of your appliquéd designs or along the patchwork seams. In this way, each design element is pronounced and the quilting is made secure. If you have many small patchwork pieces, you can stitch parallel lines across the designs. Plan these at regularly spaced intervals.

Overall quilting:

When you want to fill large areas of the background with quilting, choose a simple design. The background quilting should not interfere with the patchwork or appliqué elements. Your quilting design will depend on the top fabric.

There are several popular patterns used for background quilting. If you'd like, you can be inventive with patterns such as feathers, interlocking circles, shell or scallops, and a grid. By using a compass, you can easily create circles or scallops to the size desired. Elaborate designs must be transferred to the fabric from a pattern. Geometric prints are usually quilted with an overall grid of squares or diamonds, which is the simplest pattern. Make a grid pattern with a yardstick or masking tape for accurate spacing.

Quilting designs

Quilting designs are the patterns formed by stitches on the borders and open areas of a quilt. Circles, grids, and swirling or feather designs are most often used on traditional quilts. If you are making a quilt with alternating appliquéd and plain patches, you can repeat the outline of the appliqué in stitches on the plain patch.

Sometimes a quilted design is applied to a

center panel only, as on a bed quilt or pillow. If your panel is appliquéd the borders might be plain or quilted.

Quilting on large, open areas of fabric are not only decorative, they are practical. The quilting stitches keep the batting from slipping and shifting between the top and bottom layers.

When a quilted design is used on the borders of a quilt, for example, it often serves to frame the center design. These, often elaborate, repeat patterns are found on early quilts and, over the years, give the quilt character. Due to repeated use and washing, the fabric fades and sometimes puckers to accentuate the quilting.

The quilt designs that follow are created for a variety of borders or to be used in the center of squares. If you'd like to make a quilt, plan the border to accommodate one of the designs provided here. Whether you are a beginner or experienced quilt maker, you will find it easiest to transfer same-size patterns to your fabric so you will have the exact lines to follow.

Use these designs for other projects as well. For example, make a pillow of two contrasting fabrics. There might be a 10-inch center square of light calico with a 2-inch border of a darker print. Transfer the designs to the panel and quilt with small running stitches along the lines to create the pattern. You can have fun with these designs and when you become more experienced you might like to create your own.

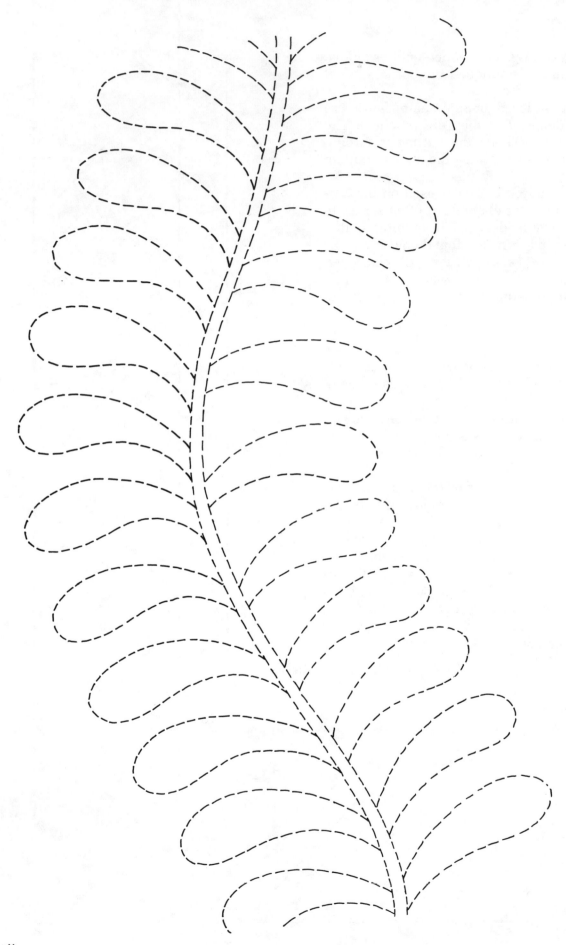

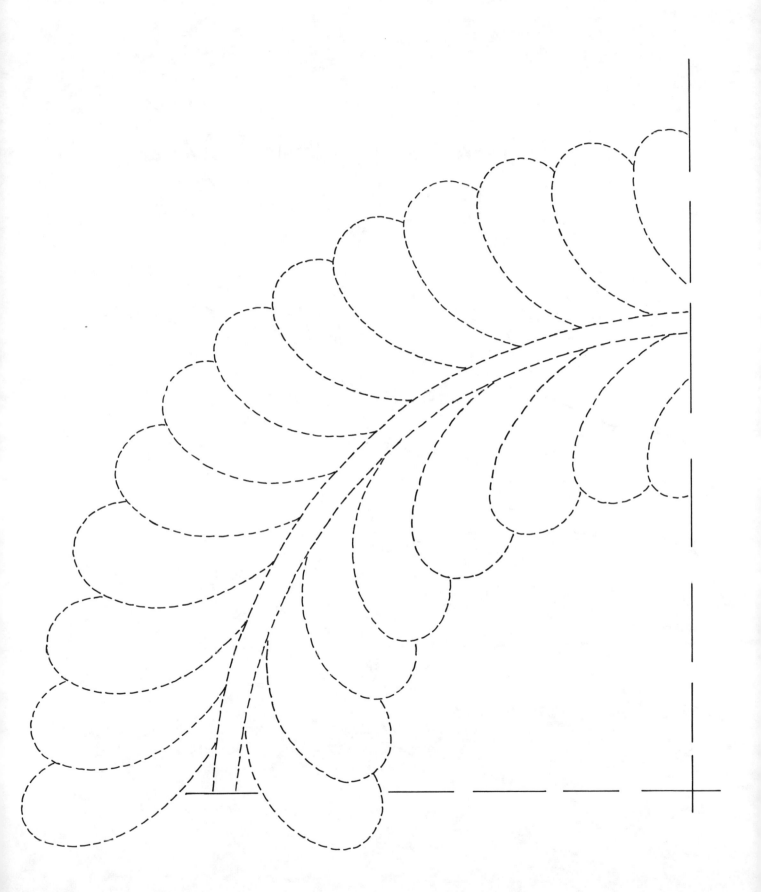

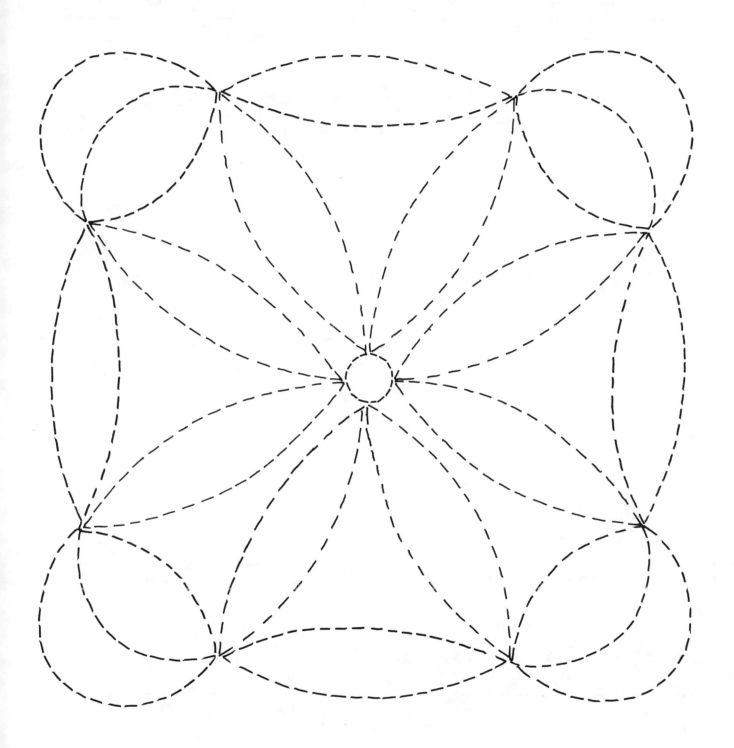

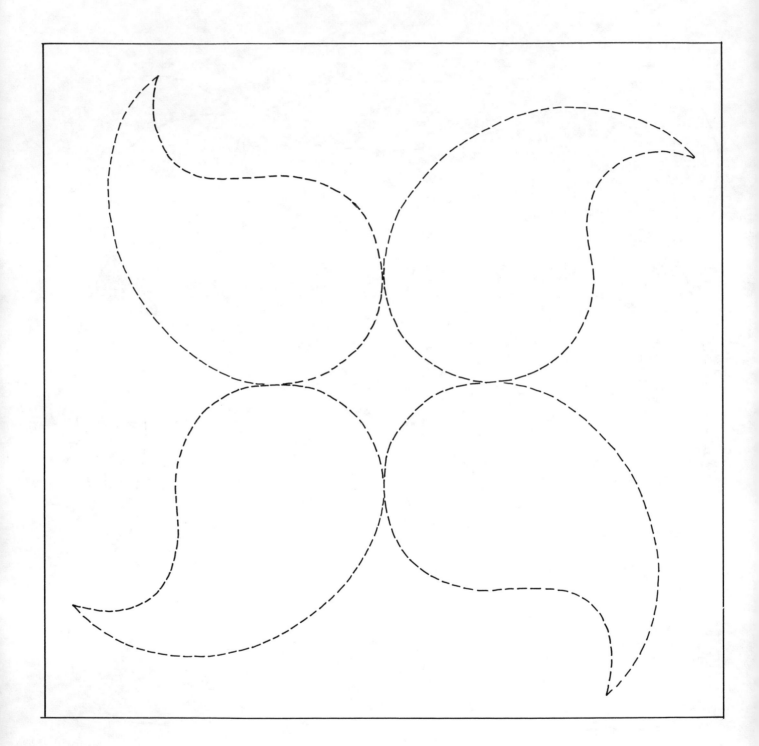

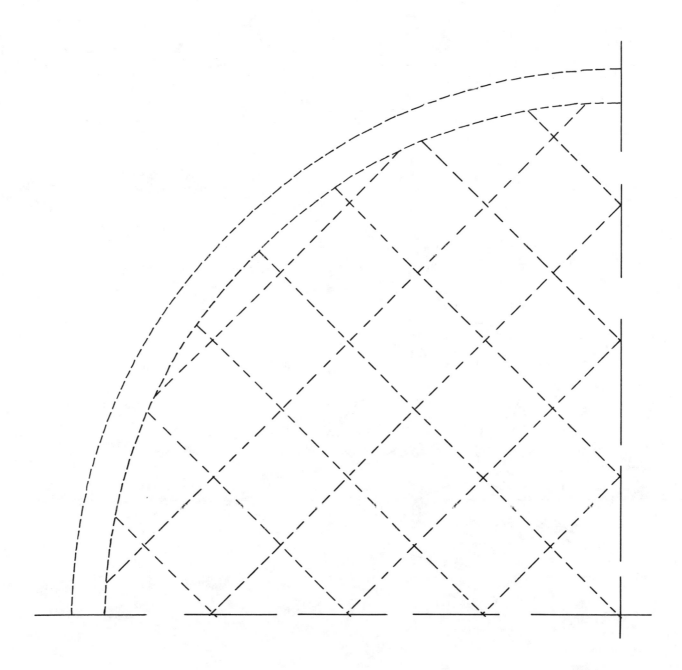

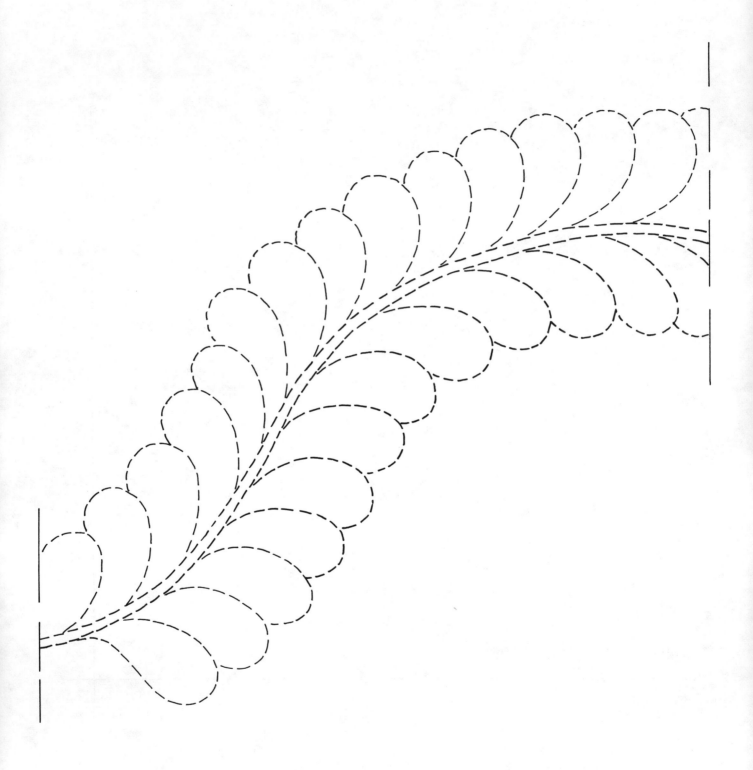

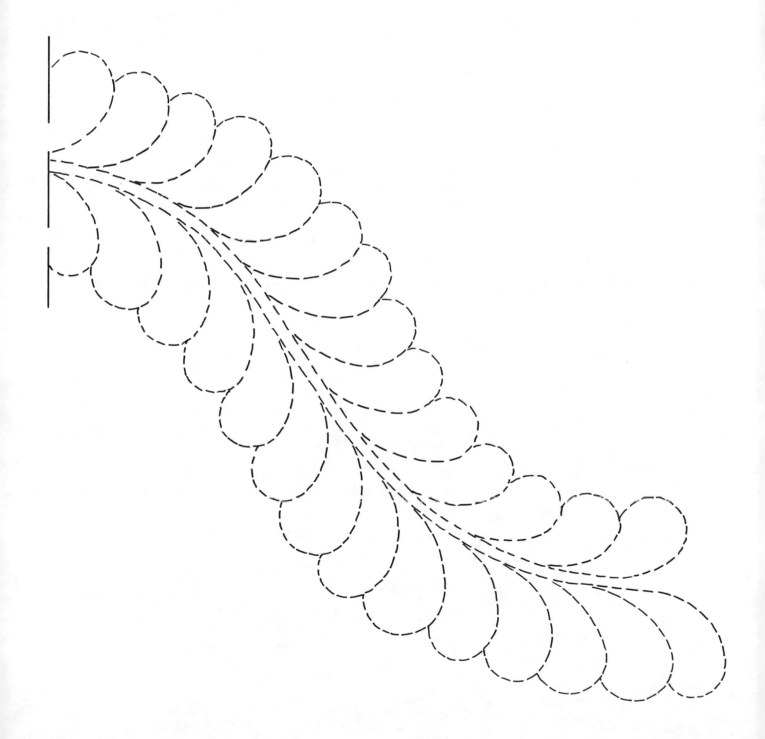

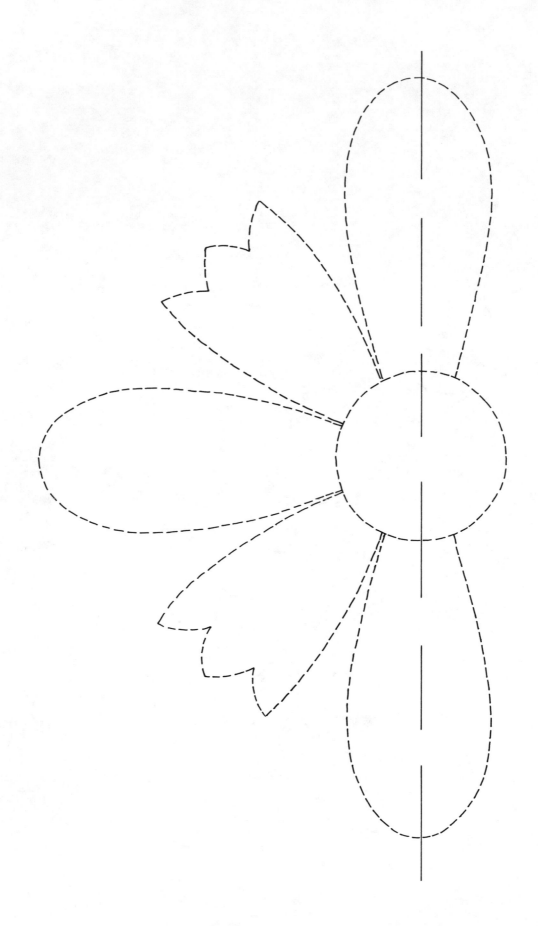

xxx

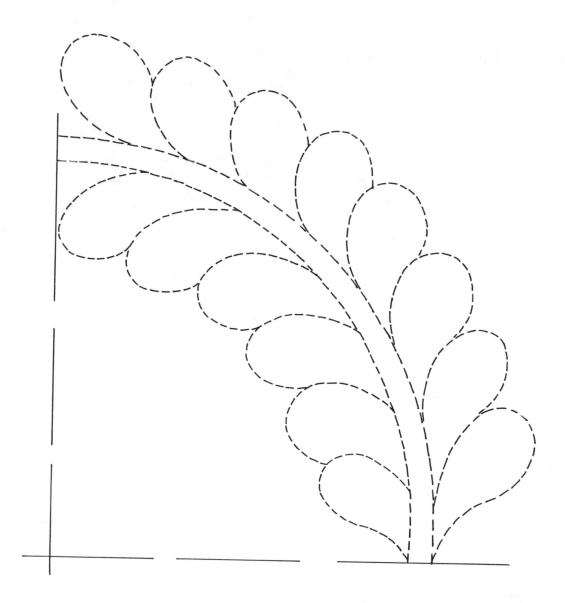

Where to find it

The materials and tools used for quilting are familiar and readily available. Since quilting has become so popular in recent years, fabric shops, art stores, and craft supply stores everywhere are responding by stocking the necessary items. Fabric shops have a wide variety of the cotton and cotton-blend prints most often sought after. These include both calicos and solids of a wide range of colors.

However, there are also small, personalized services in every part of the country. These might be shops that specifically carry quilting supplies or they might be mail-order businesses. In both cases, the owners started their businesses as an outgrowth of their hobby and they know what quilters need. Often they have developed innovative tools for the specific jobs and these are worth knowing about. I have contacted most of them and what follows is a listing of the best that my research has uncovered. If you find it difficult to locate something, one of these sources can probably help you, or you can write to me and I'll try to track it down.

Putnam is another name you often see on batting. This is what you want to look for when making an extra fluffy quilt and need that extra-thick batting. You can buy this batting in precut bed sizes or by the yard.

Quiltessentials
Box 26450
Lakewood, CO 80226

Lehman Publications, Inc.
Box 394–2
Wheatridge, CO 80034.

Lehman Publications, Inc., puts out a thirty-page catalog of reasonably priced quilting kits. There are quilts, wall hangings, pillows, totes, and more. There are all kinds of quilting aids, among them one that attracted me to check out the company. It is called Quilt-A-Peel which eliminates marking problems forever. You peel off the paper backing and stick the template on your fabric. Then quilt around the edges and remove the design to use again. Their many designs come in different sizes. The trick here is to find the design you like.

Quilt Patch
261 Main St.
Northboro, MA 01532

This company produces the sweetest little note cards with everything you need for shadow quilting a design within the oval frame of the card. The designs are simple and lovely and even a beginner should have no trouble with them. This is also a good source for 100 percent cotton prints, calicos, solids, ginghams, and polished cottons. They also carry muslin and cotton sheeting. For 400 swatches of fabric and a price list, send $3.00 and you'll find whatever you need from this distinctive quilt shop.

The Pellon Corporation has a terrific product that can be found in fabric and quilt shops. It's called Pellon Quilter's Secret and is a nonwoven, fusible material preprinted with squares and triangles to form 2- and 4-inch squares. The cutting and stitching lines are all there. You fuse this to the back of your fabric and then cut the pattern pieces. It's a simple method for mistake-proof piecing if you can use the sizes provided.

Leslie Linsley
Nantucket, Mass. 02554

Extra Special Products
P.O. Box 777
Greenville, OH 45331

This company's products are indeed extra special. Among their nifty items you'll find a plastic triangle to make perfect 8-point stars and 16-piece Dresden Plates, a multimiter to give your corners perfect miters, a key chain of 5 different angle templates, plastic sheets for templates, and grids. There are also individual appliqué kits with plastic, precut templates. A good company to know about.

Fairfield Processing Corporation
P.O. Box 1157
Danbury, CT 06810

This company's products are so familiar to quilters that you may already use it without realizing the variety available. Poly-Fil® is the brand name representing quality polyester fiber. They make pillow inserts and batting of varying thicknesses for different quilting needs. There is also an 80 percent cotton batting that is wonderful to work with. You'll find batting packaged in plastic bags with all the information needed to select the right product for your project.

Needleart Quilt
2729 Oakwood, N.E.
Grand Rapids, MI 49505

This family-run business has been operating since 1932 and supplies a catalog chock full of all kinds of hard-to-find aids, such as their raised-edge quilting thimble to keep fingers intact. You'll also find 1/4-inch craft tape for marking seams as well as water-erasable-ink marking pens. Aside from a good selection of quilting patterns they sell backing batiste at a reasonable price.

Putnam Company
P.O. Box 310
Walworth, WI 53184

PLATE 1   Calico Pot Holder, Patchwork Placemat, Chicken Little Egg Cozy Kitten Tea Cozy

PLATE 2　Butterfly Placemats

PLATE 3　Pocket Tissue Cases, Tissue Box Cover, Lingerie Bag

PLATE 4 Fence Rail
Pillow,
Dresden Plate Pillow

PLATE 5 Shoe-fly Quilt

PLATE 6   Embroidered Tote Bag, Eyeglass Case

Book One

First Steps in Quilting for You and Your Home

CALICO POT HOLDER

A patchwork pot holder is the perfect project for learning how to quilt. It is quick and easy and provides you with a feeling of satisfaction and a desire to do more. Because you can often use scrap materials, a pot holder is a good, quick, and inexpensive item to make in quantity to sell at a bazaar.

The designs used here are traditional patchwork and the finished size is 8¹/₂ × 8¹/₂ inches.

Materials

Scraps of red, blue, and yellow calico
1 piece of backing fabric 9 × 9 inches (one of the colors)
polyester batting
8 inches of ¹/₂-inch-wide ribbon to match fabric colors
thread to match fabric colors
needle

Directions

Trace each pattern piece (A, B, C, and D) and transfer to heavy paper for templates (see pages xi and xiii). Each template includes a ¹/₄-inch seam allowance.

1. Cut 4 pattern A pieces and 4 pattern B pieces from the same fabric.
2. Cut 4 pattern C pieces from the same fabric (different from pattern A and B).
3. Cut 1 pattern D piece from the third color fabric.
4. Cut a piece of polyester batting 8¹/₂ × 8¹/₂ inches.

Assembly

1. With right sides facing and long edges aligned, stitch across, joining an A piece with a C piece, leaving a ¹/₄-inch seam allowance. Press seam to one side.
2. Refer to assembly diagram and attach a B piece to each short end of the C piece. Press seams to one side. Clip corners.
3. Repeat steps 1 and 2 once more.
4. With right sides facing and edges aligned, attach an A piece with a C piece, leaving a ¹/₄-inch seam allowance. Press seam to one side.
5. With right sides facing and raw edges even, stitch the A-C piece to the center D piece. Open seam and press.
6. Repeat steps 4 and 5 on the opposite side.
7. With right sides facing and edges aligned, join all 3 sections to make the pot holder square.

Quilting

Pin the pot holder top to the polyester batting. Machine-stitch along all seam lines. Stitch across the center D patch diagonally, from corner to the opposite corner to form an X.

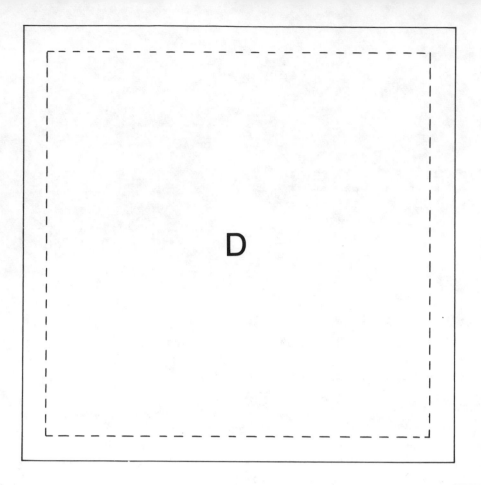
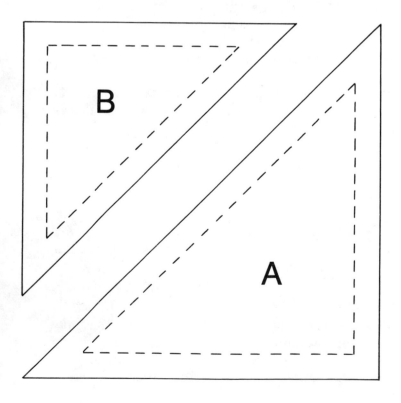
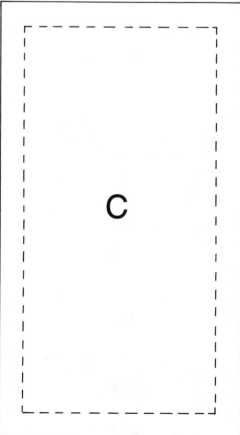

Fig. 1   Calico pot holder pattern pieces.

To finish

1. Fold the piece of ribbon in half to create a 4-inch loop for hanging. Place this on the front of the pot holder with the raw ends meeting at one corner and pin in position.
2. With right sides facing, pin backing to quilted top. Since the backing has been cut 1/2 inch larger all around, it may need trimming to line up with the raw edges of the top piece. The extra 1/2 inch is there to accommodate the thickness of the batting.
3. Stitch around 3 sides and 4 corners, leaving a 1/4-inch seam allowance. Clip off each corner.
4. Turn right side out and slip-stitch opening closed.

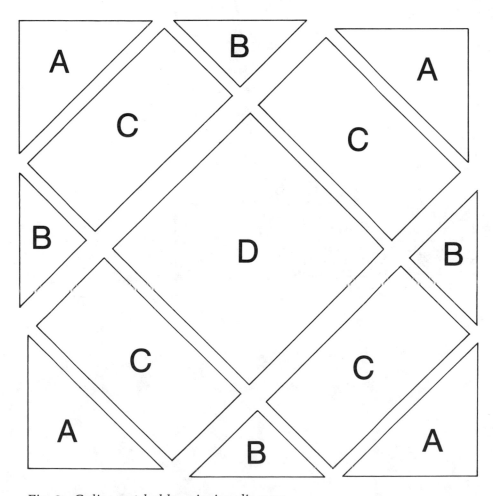

Fig. 2 Calico pot holder piecing diagram.

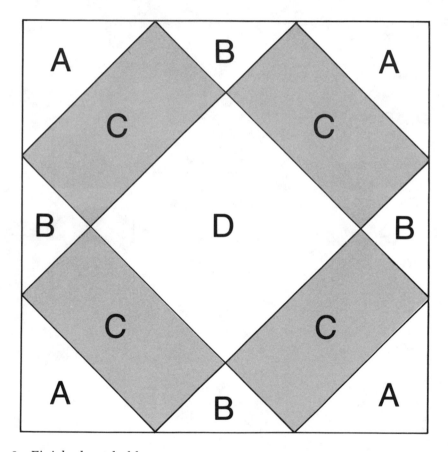

Fig. 3   Finished pot holder square.

PATCHWORK PLACE MAT

The techniques of quilting and patchwork need not be associated right away with a large quilt. In fact, it is best to learn these crafting skills on small items. A place mat is the perfect project for this, and when you are through you'll be able to vary the pattern to make a variety of matching items.

Because you are using the basic shapes of a triangle and square, there are many variations of design using the same color combinations in different ways. The finished place mat here is 12 × 16 inches and is made with bright yellow, blue, and red calico prints.

Materials (to make 4 place mats)

1 yard red calico
1/2 yard blue calico
1/2 yard yellow calico
1 yard thin quilt batting

thread to match fabric colors
tracing paper
heavy paper for template

Directions

Trace each pattern piece A and B and transfer to heavy paper to make templates (see page xiii). Use the templates to draw the number of pattern pieces needed for each fabric color as follows on next page.

Fig. 1 Patchwork place mat pattern pieces.

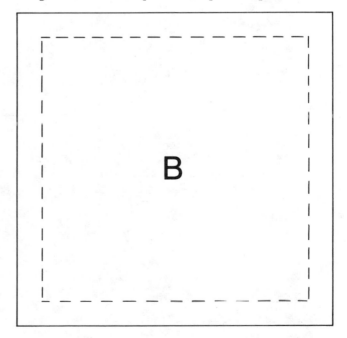

1. Cut 6 squares 2¼ × 2¼ inches from yellow fabric.
2. Cut 24 triangles from blue fabric.
3. Cut 1 rectangular piece 8½ × 12½ inches from red fabric.
4. Cut backing piece 12½ × 16½ inches from red fabric.
5. Cut quilt batting 12 × 16 inches.

To assemble

(Refer to assembly diagram)

1. With right sides facing and raw edges aligned, pin blue triangle pieces to one side of each of the yellow squares.
2. Stitch together before pinning the next triangle. Trim corners where they ex-tend beyond fabric edge. Open seams and press.
3. Continue to join a triangle to each side of the squares until you have 6 blue-and-yellow-patchwork squares for each place mat.
4. With right sides facing and raw edges aligned, join 3 patchwork squares together to form a row. Open seams and press. Repeat with remaining 3 squares.
5. With right sides facing and raw edges aligned, stitch one row of patchwork squares to the long edge of the red center rectangle piece. Open seams and press.
6. Repeat on opposite side to complete the top of the place mat.

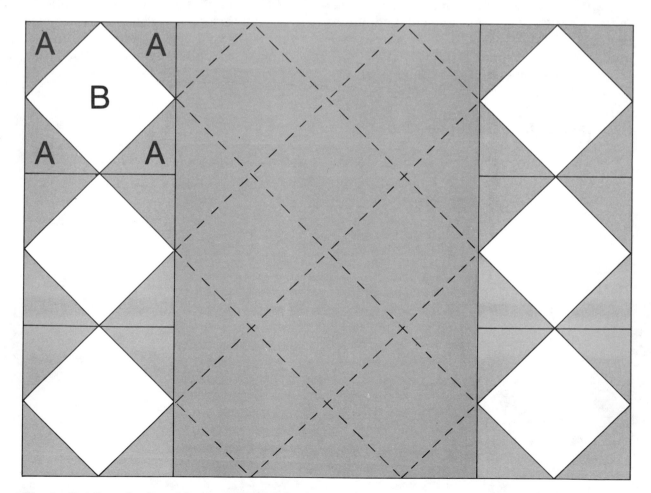

Fig. 2 *Patchwork place mat assembly diagram.*

8

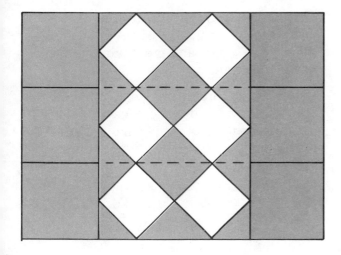
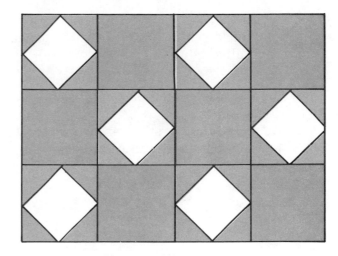
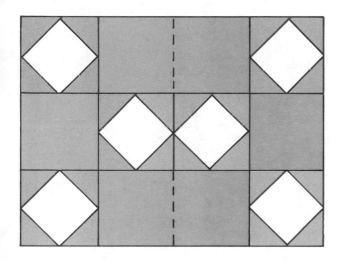
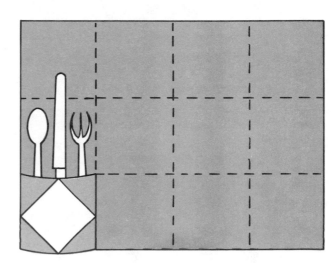

Fig. 3 Many variations are possible using the same pattern pieces.

To quilt

Using a light pencil and ruler, mark off a grid with 2-inch spaces between the lines across the red center of the place mat. These lines should match up with the points of each square on the side panels.

1. Pin the top of the place mat to the quilt batting.
2. Using blue thread in your sewing machine and a stitch length set at approximately 4 for a long stitch, sew along marked lines on the red calico to machine-quilt.
3. With blue thread stitch 1/8 inch inside seam line of each blue triangle.
4. Change to yellow thread and stitch along inside edge of each square patch close to the seam line. These stitch lines define the patchwork and create the quilting on the place mat. All stitches can be done by hand if desired, but machine stitching is quicker and easier and the long stitches create a uniform look.

9

To finish

Cut a backing piece 12½ × 16½ inches from red calico fabric.

1. Pin the right side of the backing over the top right side of the place mat so all raw edges match.
2. Using red thread, stitch around all sides, leaving one short end of the red center panel (8 inches) open for turning.

3. Clip off each corner and turn right side out. Turn the 8 inches of raw edges to the inside ¼ inch and press. Pin opening edges together.

4. Using blue thread in your machine, stitch around the outside edge of the entire place mat just inside the seam allowance. Press and trim away all thread ends.

CHICKEN LITTLE EGG COZY

Keep your soft boiled eggs warm with a Chicken Little egg cozy. These bright yellow and red covers slip over the egg cup and add a cheerful note to your morning table. When not serving breakfast, cover a little sugar bowl on a kitchen shelf or just keep the egg cozy hanging where it can be seen. This is a good bazaar project as you can make many of them quickly and from scraps of leftover fabrics.

Materials

Piece of yellow fabric 8 × 12 inches
scrap of black felt for eye
scrap of red felt for beak
2 pieces of quilt batting 4 × 6 inches
1 yard of 1/2-inch-wide double-fold red
    bias binding
1 skein red embroidery floss
tape
needles (1 embroidery, 1 regular)
tracing paper
hard pencil
white glue

Directions

Trace the egg cozy pattern from the book and pin to the yellow fabric. Cut out 4 pattern pieces without seam allowance. Cut 2 pieces of batting the same size as the pattern.

1. Tape the traced pattern to a window-pane and tape one piece of yellow fabric over the tracing.
2. Using a hard pencil (a soft pencil will smudge the fabric), trace the chicken feathers and eye onto the fabric.

To quilt

Pin the traced fabric piece to one piece of quilt batting. If the batting is showing beyond the fabric edges, trim all around so edges match.

1. Cut a length of embroidery floss about 18 inches long and separate the strands. Using 3 strands in the embroidery needle, bring it up through the batting side to the beginning of one drawn line on the fabric. Leave about 2 inches of tail on the underside, but do not make a knot in the thread.
2. Using a backstitch, follow the outline of the pencil markings to quilt the feathered body of the chicken.
3. When finished, weave the floss end under several stitches on the underside of the batting to secure. Do not make a knot at the end.

To assemble
1. Pin the embroidered piece to a corresponding yellow piece of fabric (lining) with the batting between.
2. With right sides out, pin the 2 remaining patterns together with batting between.

3. Pin the embroidered front piece to the back piece all around the curved edge. Leave the bottom edges free.
4. Using the bias binding, begin at one bottom edge and pin around the raw, curved edges, joining the back and front of the egg cozy.

To finish
1. Using matching thread, blindstitch around the binding to finish the curved edge.
2. Pin the binding around the bottom raw edges to secure the outside, batting, and lining. Stitch around the inside edge of the binding to finish.
3. Cut a circle from the black felt the same size as the eye pattern and glue or stitch it in position on the embroidered side of the egg cozy.
5. Cut a red felt beak, using the pattern provided, and stitch in position from the back side of the egg cozy.

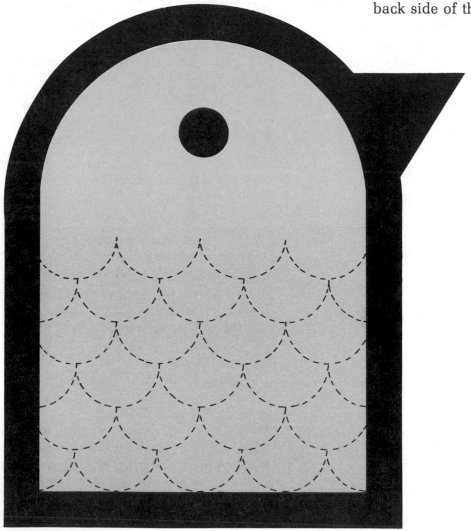

Fig. 1 Egg cozy pattern.

*Fig. 2   To make rooster, add yellow felt beak
and red crop.*

13

Fig. 3. To make penguin, appliqué black felt on white fabric and use yellow felt for beak.

KITTEN TEA COZY

Decorate your kitchen and keep your teapot hot at the same time. This darling, sleeping kitten is the perfect shape for a quilted tea cozy. Outlined in red on a bright yellow background, the project is designed for quick and easy crafting and will cheer up any corner of your kitchen where it is used.

Materials

1/3 yard 45-inch-wide yellow fabric
2 pieces of quilt batting 8 1/2 × 11 inches
1 package double-fold, 1/2-inch-wide red bias binding
1 skein red embroidery floss
tape
embroidery needle
tracing paper
ruler
hard pencil

Directions

Enlarge the pattern according to directions on page xiii. Each square equals 1 inch. The kitten design is shown full-size.

1. Place the pattern on the yellow fabric and cut out the shape of the tea cozy 4 times. Two pieces will be used for the front and back outside and 2 for the lining.

2. Tape the kitten design to a windowpane. Tape one piece of yellow fabric over the design so that the kitten is positioned in the center of the fabric. You should be able to see the design through the fabric.

3. Using the hard pencil (a soft pencil will smudge the fabric), outline the kitten and details on the body.

To quilt

Pin the traced fabric piece to one piece of quilt batting all around the edges. Place a pin in the center to hold fabric and batting together. Trim the batting around the outer edge if it is larger than the fabric.

1. Separate the strands of an 18-inch length of embroidery floss. Using only 3 strands, thread the embroidery needle, but do not make a knot at one end as you would normally do when sewing by hand.

2. Beginning on the batting side, bring the needle through the fabric at the inside start of the cat's tail. Leave approximately 2 inches of floss free on the underside.

3. Using a backstitch, follow the outline of your pencil markings to quilt the kitten's body and all the details.

4. When finished, weave the floss end under several stitches on the underside of the batting to secure. Do not make a knot at the end.

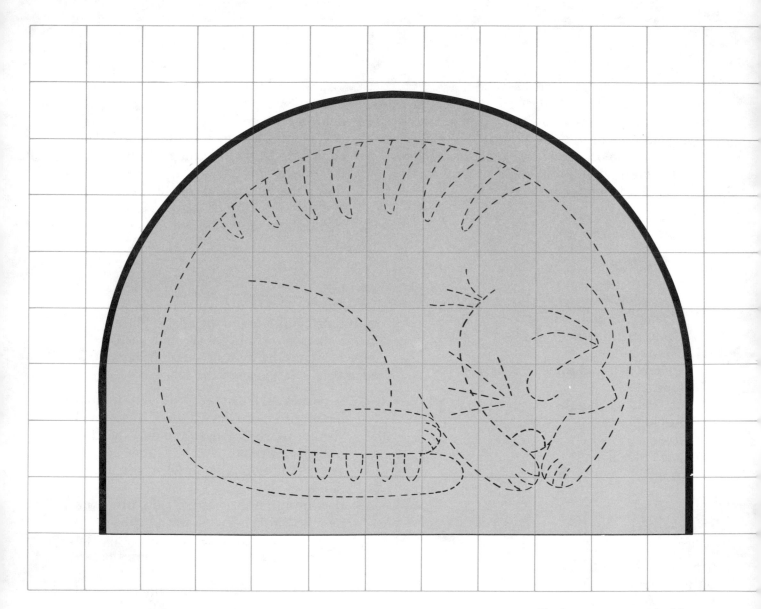

Each square equals 1″

Fig. 1 Kitten tea cozy pattern.

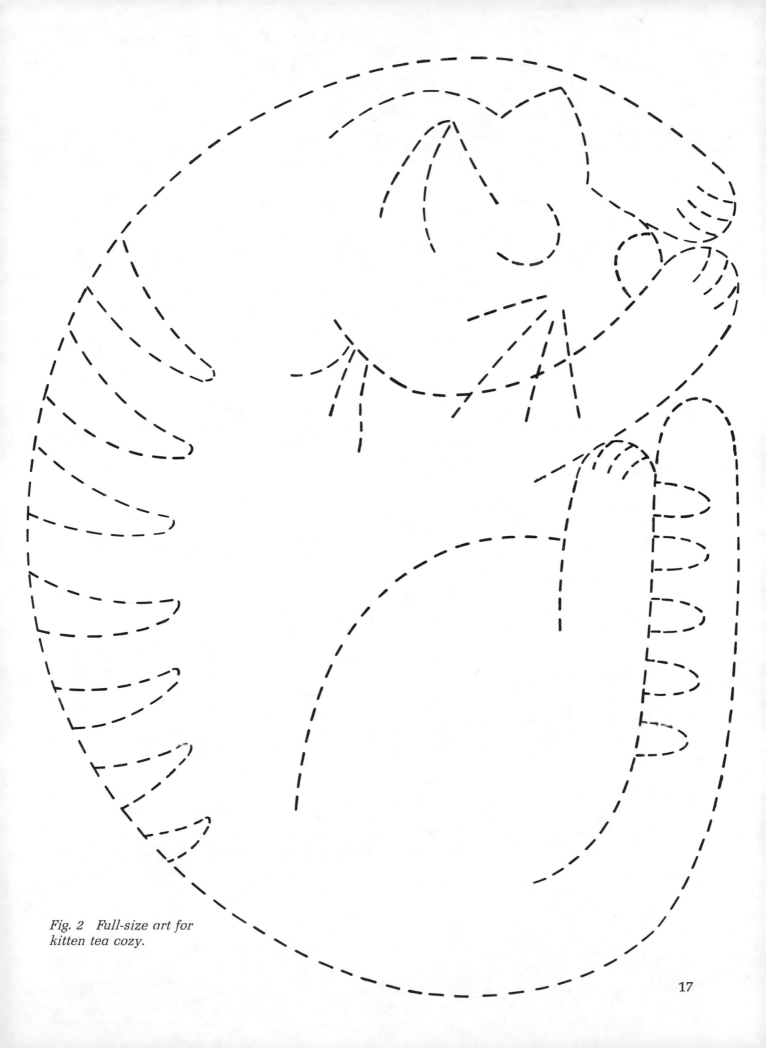

Fig. 2 Full-size art for kitten tea cozy.

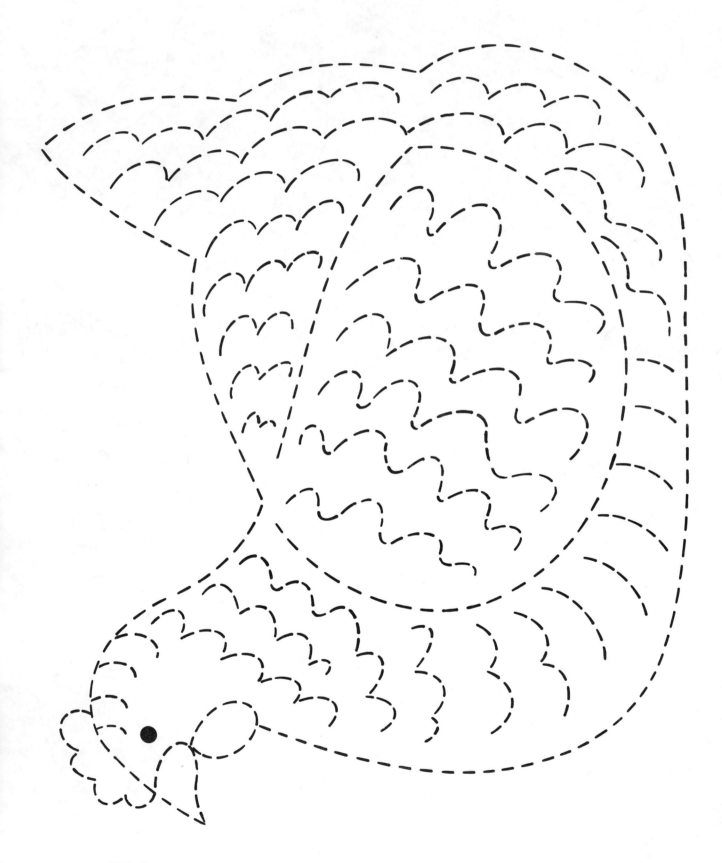

Fig. 3 Full-size art for hen tea cozy.

To assemble

1. Baste the embroidered front to a corresponding yellow piece of fabric (lining) with the batting between.
2. With right sides out, baste together the 2 remaining cozy pattern pieces with batting between.
3. Pin the embroidered front piece to the back all around the curved edge. Leave the bottom edges free.
4. Using the bias binding, begin at one bottom edge and pin around the raw, curved edges, joining the back and front of the tea cozy.

To finish

1. Using matching thread, blindstitch around the binding to finish the curved edge.
2. Pin the binding around the bottom raw edges to secure the outside, batting, and lining. Stitch around the inside edge of the binding to finish.
3. Remove all basting stitches.
4. Cut a 2-inch strip of bias binding and fold in half lengthwise. Secure with a few stitches at the back of the center top for easy removal of the tea cozy from your teapot.

BUTTERFLY PLACE MATS

One calico print is used in 2 different colors for place mats with butterfly appliqués. One place mat has a dark, navy blue mat with pink butterflies. The other is made with pink fabric and the butterfly appliqués are made from navy blue print. This is a nice way to have variety within matching sets for your table setting.

A simple shape is the easiest one for appliqués until you are more experienced with this technique of applying one fabric to another. Small pieces are more difficult to work with than larger ones. The butterflies are made from 2 identical, curved pieces. The decorative backstitch done with embroidery thread creates the quilting and adds details to the appliqué. The finished size of each place mat is $11\frac{1}{2} \times 16$ inches.

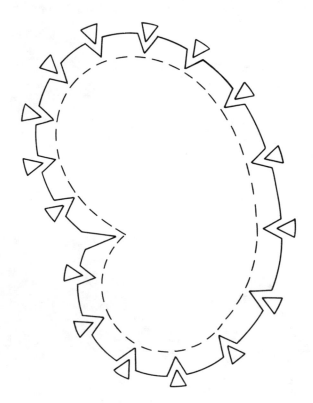

Fig. 1   Clip around edges of butterfly appliqué.

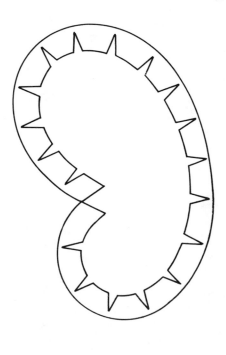

Fig. 2   Fold edges over template.

Materials (for 2 place mats)

1/2 yard 36-inch-wide pink calico
1/2 yard 36-inch-wide navy blue calico
thin quilt batting
thread to match fabric colors
1 skein each of pink and blue embroidery
   floss
embroidery needle
tracing paper
heavy paper for template
dressmaker's (carbon) paper

Directions

1. Trace pattern pieces A and B (including C) and transfer to heavy paper for templates (see page xiii for details).
2. Cut the following pieces of fabric:
   Navy blue:
      11½ × 13 inches (cut 1)
      13 × 17½ inches (cut 1)

Pink:
   11½ × 16 inches (cut 1)
   13 × 17½ inches (cut 1)

3. Place template A on the navy fabric and trace around the shape 7 times, leaving room between each for a 3/8-inch seam allowance. Repeat with B template.
4. Repeat for the pink pieces (7).

To prepare appliqués

1. Cut out each pattern piece with 3/8-inch seam allowance.
2. Clip around the edges 1/4 inch into the seam allowance (see Fig. 1).
3. Position the template on the wrong side of the fabric and press the edges of the appliqué over the edges of the template.
4. Remove the template and press the turned edges with a medium-hot iron to set them in place. As you can see from the diagram, 2 of the butterfly appliqués are only partially used, as they "fly" off the edges of the place mat. It is easiest, however, to make full appliqués and cut away the excess after they have been pinned to the fabric background. It is a bit more work but ensures accuracy.

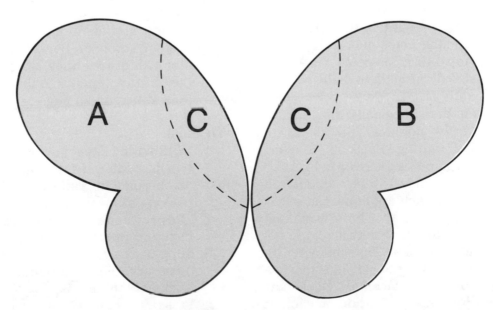

Fig. 3 Butterfly place mat appliqué pattern.

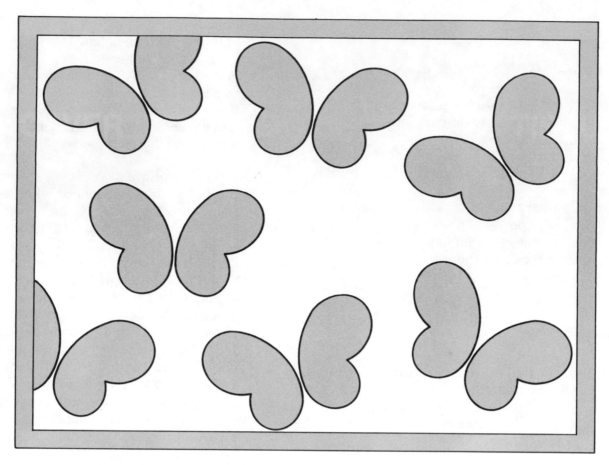

Fig. 4   Butterfly place mat layout.

To quilt

1. Cut a piece of quilt batting 11½ × 16 inches for each place mat.
2. Pin the top fabric piece to the batting and baste all around to hold in place while quilting.
3. Following the placement diagram, pin the butterfly appliqué pieces to the fabric and batting. Each set of wings should be placed as shown in Fig. 4.
4. Machine- or hand-stitch around the outer edge of each appliqué. Cut excess appliqué piece away where it overlaps the edge of the place mat.
5. Now that you have finished with the template, cut away the C piece to use as a guide for detail placement on each ap-pliqué. Hold this in position on each ap-pliqué and draw a light pencil line as a stitch guide. Remove the template.
6. Using 3 strands of embroidery floss and a stem stitch or backstitch, embroider along all drawn lines, with blue floss on the pink appliqués and pink on the navy. (See stitch guide, page xix.)

To finish

1. With wrong sides facing and batting be-tween, center the top appliquéd fabric on the backing, allowing 1½ inches of backing all around.
2. Turn raw edges of backing forward ¼ inch and press.
3. Turn backing edges forward to the top piece and pin all around. Machine-sew or slip-stitch to finish the ½-inch border. Press.

Fig. 5   Vine place mat layout.

Fig. 6   Flower place mat layout.

POCKET TISSUE CASE

A little item such as this takes a small amount of fabric and very little time to make. For these reasons it is a perfect, last-minute gift or bazaar item. You can make several from scraps of fabric in a variety of fabric color and print combinations.

Any fabric can be quilted for this project, but I recommend a small, overall print, or a busy print without large areas of solid background. A solid fabric can also be used, in which case you might like to create a quilting pattern for interest on the fabric.

Materials

1/4 yard cotton print fabric
thin quilt batting
1 × 13-inch strip of contrasting fabric or
    ribbon
thread
small package of tissues

Fig. 1   Finished pocket tissue case.

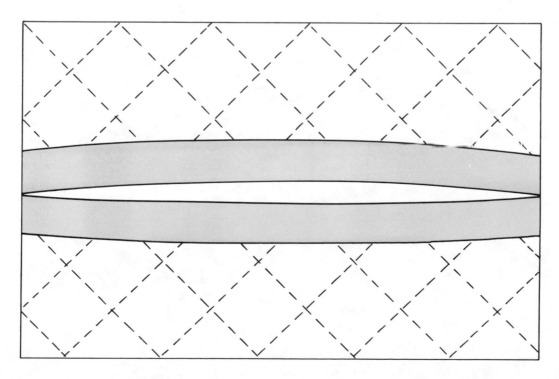

Directions

1. Cut 2 pieces of fabric $6\frac{1}{2} \times 7$ inches.
2. Cut a piece of batting $6 \times 6\frac{1}{2}$ inches.
3. With wrong sides facing and batting between, pin the 2 pieces of fabric together.
4. If the fabric has a striped, checked, or geometric pattern, stitch along the lines of the print to quilt. If the fabric is a floral print, quilt around the outline of the design. If the fabric is an overall print or solid, mark a grid of evenly spaced lines, approximately $\frac{1}{2}$ inch, for example. Stitch along these premarked lines.
5. Cut the narrow strip of fabric in half so you have 2 pieces $1 \times 6\frac{1}{2}$ inches.
6. Turn each long edge of each strip under $\frac{1}{4}$ inch and press. Fold each strip in half lengthwise and press. You now have 2 strips $\frac{1}{2} \times 6\frac{1}{2}$ inches.
7. Encase both $6\frac{1}{2}$-inch edges of the quilted fabric within the fabric strips and pin. Stitch together at each end.
8. With right sides facing, fold the bound edges in so they meet in the center. Pin at each end.
9. Stitch across the raw edges, leaving a $\frac{5}{8}$-inch seam allowance. Trim the seams close to the stitch line and clip the corners.
10. Turn right side out and press. Slip a small traveling package of tissues into the case.

TISSUE BOX COVER

This is a perfect complement to any room. Cover a tissue box to match a bathroom wallpaper or fabric in a bedroom. Laura Ashley's cotton print is used here for a delicate country look, perfect for quilting.

A good way to learn how to quilt is by making a small item with fabric that has a small symmetrical print, checks, stripes, or a grid. In this way you simply follow the lines of the design as a guide. Similarly, a floral print can be quilted by stitching around each design element. This can be done by machine or hand and enables you to get the feel of the quilting process without committing yourself to a large project right away.

Materials

1/4 yard printed fabric
thin quilt batting
1 yard piping in a color to match
embroidery floss to match a color in the fabric
quilting needle
tissue box

Directions

The tissue box is used as your template for measuring fabric pieces. Therefore, you can use these directions for covering any size box, the only variable will be the amount of fabric used.

1. Begin by cutting 1 piece of fabric to fit the top of the box, adding 1/2 inch all around.
2. Measure the perimeter and height of the box and cut 1 strip of fabric to these dimensions, adding 1/2 inch all around. This piece wraps around the sides, front, and back.
3. Cut a piece of batting 1/2 inch smaller all around for each piece of fabric.
4. If there are no guidelines (that is, grid, checks, stripes) on your fabric, rule off evenly spaced horizontal and vertical lines, using a ruler and hard pencil or water-soluble marker (see page xi).
5. Pin the corresponding batting piece to the wrong side of each fabric piece.
6. Remove the top opening piece from the tissue box. Using this as your template, center it on the top fabric piece with batting and mark around it with a pencil (see Fig. 1). Working 1/2 inch inside the lines you just drew, cut out an opening on the fabric and batting. Notch curved edges (see Fig. 2).
7. Cut a piece of fabric on the bias, 1 inch wide and long enough to fit around the hole opening plus an extra 1/2 inch. Turn the long edges under 1/4 inch and press. Turn 1 short end under 1/4 inch and press. Fold the strip in half lengthwise and press.
8. Encase the raw edge of the hole opening in the bias strip overlapping ends where they meet. Stitch around.

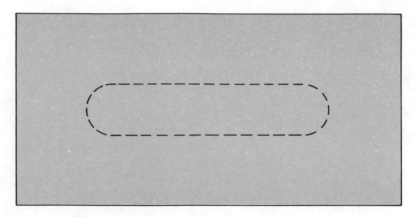

Fig. 1 Remove hole from tissue box to use as template on fabric.

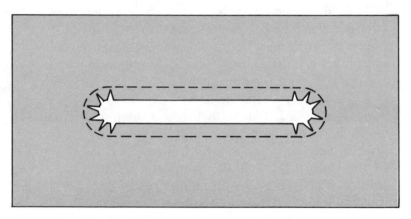

Fig. 2 Cut tissue box opening and notch curves.

To quilt

There are different ways to quilt the fabric. You can use embroidery thread and a backstitch as shown on this project. In this case I chose a bright green thread to match the leaves of the roses in the print. The background of this fabric is beige and the embroidered, green stitches contrast nicely and add to the design.

You can also machine-quilt, using a matching thread on the fabric. In this way, the dimensional quality of the quilting will be more obvious than the stitches. Or, you can choose a matching or contrasting thread and quilt by hand, using a small running stitch. Some people want to save time by using the machine-quilting method. Others prefer lap work and like to quilt by hand. Since the item is so small, you may choose to embroider by hand using the contrasting embroidery thread. The effect is quite pretty.

1. If using embroidery floss, use 3 strands only and quilt along the premarked lines of your fabric with a small backstitch. For each panel, begin from the back, make a small knot, and pull the thread through the batting and fabric. Try to keep your stitches even and taut without bunching the fabric as you sew.

2. If stitching on the machine, set the stitch-length dial for a longer stitch than

one you would use for regular seam stitching, but not as loose as for a basting stitch. This will simulate a hand-stitched look. Do not allow stitching to run into the seam allowance.

To assemble

1. With right sides facing and edges aligned, join the short ends of the side-piece, leaving a 1/2-inch seam allowance (see Fig. 3).
2. With raw edges aligned, pin the piping around the outer edge of the top piece of fabric. Stitch around.
3. With right sides facing and piping between, pin and join the top and side sections (see Fig. 3).
4. Trim all seam allowance as close to the stitching line as possible. Turn right side out and slip over the tissue box.
5. Pull the cover down so it fits comfortably over the box and turn the raw edge under 1/4 inch all around the bottom of the cover. Pin in place.
6. Remove the cover and stitch around the bottom edge. Replace on the tissue box.

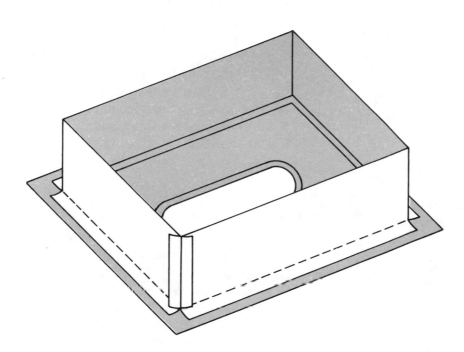

Fig. 3 Join top and sides of tissue box.

LINGERIE BAG

Any small, overall printed fabric can be quilted. The evenly spaced Laura Ashley print is divided into a 3/4-inch grid with each little design outlined in a square. Simply rule off the fabric with lines that conform to the fabric pattern.

This quilted bag is machine-stitched in the background color of the fabric. The lining is solid blue to match the print and there is an inside pocket as well. The finished size is approximately 9 × 13 inches, which is ample for a clutch purse when the bag is not used to hold lingerie.

Materials

1/2 yard 45-inch-wide printed fabric
1/2 yard (any width) solid fabric in color to match print
quilt batting
thread to match fabric
needle
tracing paper
ruler
hard pencil
snap for closure

Directions (All directions include 1/4-inch seam allowance.)

Trace pattern piece A. This is the pattern for the sidepieces of the bag. A template isn't necessary as you can use the paper pattern to cut the 2 pieces needed.

1. Pin the pattern to the printed fabric and cut 2 pieces. Repeat on lining fabric.
2. From the printed fabric, cut pieces in the following sizes:
   14 × 27 1/2 inches for main piece
   10 1/2 × 14 inches for flap lining
3. From solid fabric, cut pieces in the following sizes:
   7 1/2 × 12 3/4 inches for pocket
   12 3/4 × 16 inches for main lining piece
4. Cut batting 14 × 27 1/2 inches.
5. Cut 2 pieces of batting, using pattern piece A as a guide. Cut away seam allowance.

To quilt

1. Use a ruler to mark off a grid over the main fabric piece 14 × 27 1/2 inches.
2. Pin batting to back of main piece and machine-stitch along all drawn lines, stopping 1/4 inch from fabric edges.
3. Rule off lines on flap lining fabric and machine-stitch without batting.
4. Rule off lines on sidepieces A and pin to corresponding batting pieces.
5. Stitch along marked lines.

To assemble

1. Place main fabric piece right side up, lengthwise on work surface.
2. With right sides facing and raw edges

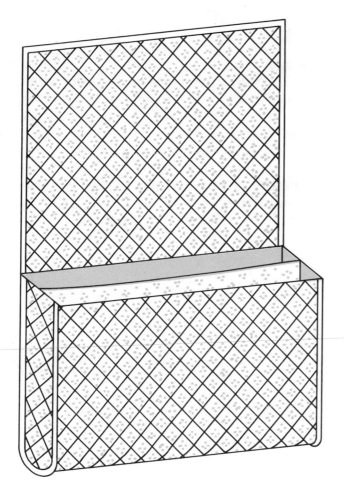

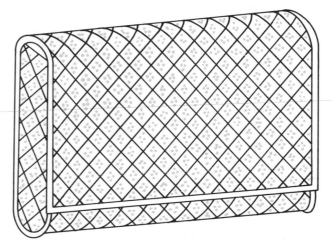

Fig. 1 Use fabric print as guide
for diagonal quilting.

aligned, pin flap lining piece to one short
end of main piece.

3. Stitch around the 3 outside edges. Clip
   corners.
4. Clip around the curve of the sidepieces
   A in the seam allowance.
5. Place curved piece face down on the
   edge of the short end of the fabric, with
   curve in center of the main piece (see
   Fig. 2) and pin along outside edge.
6. Fold right-hand edge of main piece forward and continue to pin curve of side-
   piece and long edge, with right sides facing. Repeat on opposite edge to set
   sidepieces A in place. Stitch around.
7. Turn lining and main section right side
   out and press.

Lining

1. With right side up, pin pocket piece to
   front of lining, 1/2 inch from one, short
   end.
2. With right sides facing and raw edges
   aligned, join sidepieces A as for outside,
   with pocket piece between, at seam line.
   Stitch across bottom edge of pocket.
3. Turn top edge of lining 1/4 inch to wrong
   side of fabric and press. Turn raw edge
   of main bag piece to inside 1/4 inch and
   press.
4. Slip lining into bag and slip-stitch
   around top edges to join outside and lining and to hide raw edge of inside flap.

31

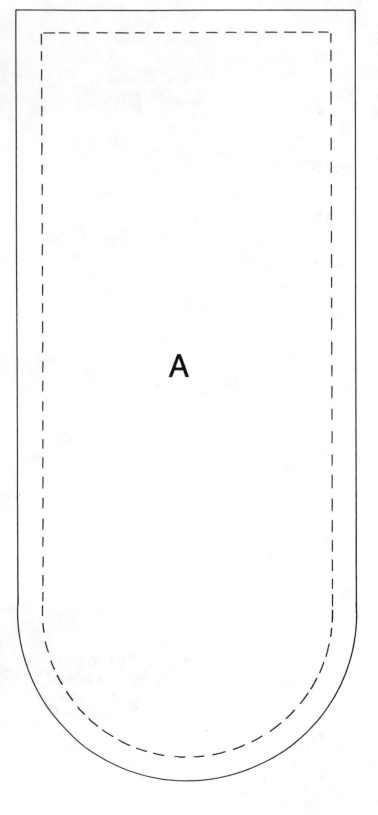

To finish

Stitch 1/2 inch from edge around outer edge of flap. Pin sides and outer bag together 1/2 inch in from seam line. Stitch around outside, curved piece A for a finished, quilted edge.

Place a snap closure on the inside, center edge of the flap. Fold forward and place corresponding snap piece on the bag. You can also use a button with a loop closing or a piece of Velcro in place of the snap.

Fig. 2 Lingerie bag side pattern.

FENCE RAIL PILLOW

The Fence Rail design is a familiar one to quilt makers. Laura Ashley fabric is used here in a combination of light, medium, and dark hues. The small, overall prints are all different but work well together.

There are 9 squares of identical strips of 3 different fabric patterns. Each strip is $1^1/2 \times 4^1/2$ inches and, when joined, create a $4^1/2$-inch square. Each of these squares is placed in such a way that they form a light/dark pattern when all 9 are joined together.

The easiest way to make this project is with the "strip method," sometimes known as assembly-line quilting. It eliminates much piecing and is especially timesaving when you are working on a large item such as a quilt. You simply stitch the full-length strips together and cut them at evenly spaced intervals. They are then arranged according to the diagram.

Materials

All fabric must be 45 inches wide. You will need a 2-inch-wide piece of 3 different fabrics: light, medium, and dark.

$13^1/2 \times 13^1/2$-inch piece of fabric for backing

thin quilt batting

Poly-Fil® stuffing

$1^1/2$ yards piping

thread to match fabric colors

Directions

Begin by cutting 3 strips of each fabric 2×45 inches long.

1. With right sides facing and raw edges aligned, stitch a light and dark strip together. Open seams and press.
2. Join the medium-shade fabric to the light fabric in the same way.
3. Cut across the 3 strips every 5 inches to make 9 squares.

Fig. 1 Fence Rail pillow assembly diagram.

To assemble

1. With right sides facing and raw edges aligned, follow the assembly diagram and stitch 3 squares together to form a row. Repeat 2 more times.
2. Join all rows according to the diagram.
3. Press all seams toward the darker fabric if any seam allowance shows through the light fabric.

To quilt

1. Cut the thin quilt batting 13 inches square and baste to the back of the pieced fabric.
2. Using a single strand of thread in a color to match each fabric background, take even running stitches approximately 1/8 inch inside each seam line.
3. Remove basting stitches.

To finish

1. With raw edges aligned, pin the piping around the front top of the pillow.
2. With right sides facing, pin backing piece to front of pieced top fabric.
3. Using the piping stitches as a guide (on the wrong side), stitch around 3 sides

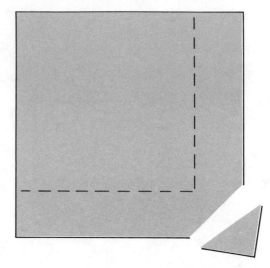

Fig. 2   Trim corners before turning pillow.

and 4 corners of the fabric, leaving 1/4-inch seam allowance.
4. Clip corners and turn pillow right side out. Press.
5. Stuff the pillow with Poly-Fil®. Use a blunt, pointed object, such as a crochet hook or the end of an artist's brush, to get the stuffing into corners.
6. Slip-stitch opening closed.

34

DRESDEN PLATE PILLOW

Many quilt patterns are created with circles and parts of circles pieced together and appliquéd to a fabric background. The Dresden Plate is a good example of a popular design employing this technique. It is often found on pillows as well as on quilts.

The design is made up of 8 pieces, and the pieces are joined with straight seams. Only the outer curved edges are turned and the pieced design is applied as one appliqué. The circle is a separate piece, appliquéd over the center where each piece meets.

Calico fabric comes in a variety of country prints and a wide range of colors that work well together. You can make the project to match almost any decorating scheme, as calico seems to fit with most styles of furnishing. Finished pillow is 14 × 14 inches.

Materials

½ yard dark brown calico
½ yard white fabric
scraps of tan, rose, and white calico prints
quilt batting
thread to match fabric
needle
tracing paper
heavy paper for template
14 × 14 inch pillow form

Directions

Trace each pattern piece A and B and transfer to heavy paper for template (see page xiii). Seam allowance of ¼ inch is included on each template pattern.

1. Using template A, draw around and cut out 4 pieces from the tan calico, 2 pieces from the rose calico, and 2 from the dark brown calico.
2. Using template B, draw around and cut out 1 piece from the white calico.
3. Cut a piece of white fabric 14½ × 14½ inches for the background.
4. With right sides facing and raw edges aligned, join a dark brown A piece to a tan A piece. Open seams and press. Repeat with another tan piece on the opposite side of the dark brown piece. Next, join a rose piece A to each tan piece, followed by a tan A piece to each edge of a rose piece. End the circle with a brown A piece. (See piecing diagram.) Open all seams and press.
5. Clip around all curved edges to the seam line.

To appliqué
1. Cut away the seam allowance from the template A piece.
2. With wrong side up, place the pieced circle on an ironing board. Position the template A on each calico section and

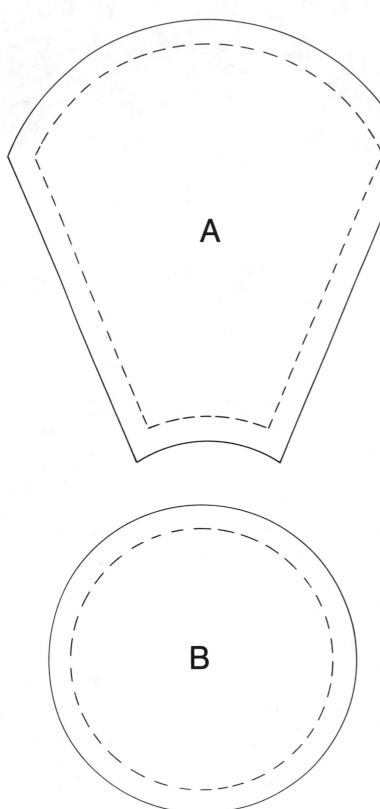

Fig. 1   Dresden Plate pattern pieces.

press the curved edge over the curved edge of the template. Remove the template and iron over the turned edge once more.

3. Cut away the seam allowance from the circle template B. Place the white calico circle wrong side up on ironing board and center the template on the fabric.

4. Clip around in the seam allowance and turn raw edges over the edges of the template all around. Press and remove template. Press again.

5. Machine-stitch around all turned edges of Dresden Plate appliqué and center piece.

6. Center the scalloped appliqué on the white background fabric and pin in position.

7. Center the fabric circle over all raw edges in the center of the appliqué and pin in position.

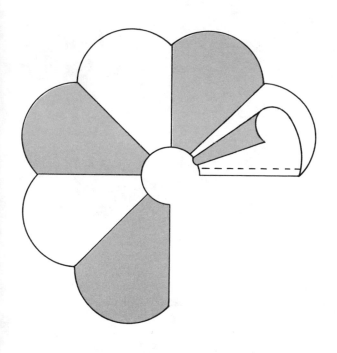

Fig. 2 *Piecing diagram for Dresden Plate.*

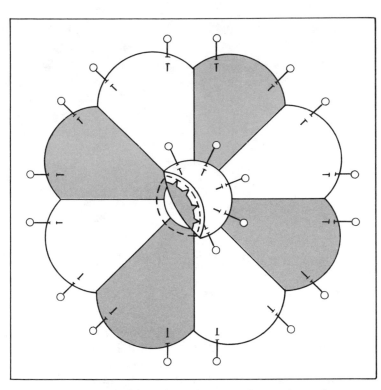

Fig. 3 *Turn edges of appliqué under and stitch to background fabric.*

8. Blindstitch around all outside edges and edge of circle.

To quilt

1. Cut batting piece 14 × 14 inches and pin to the back of the pillow top.
2. Using color thread for each fabric section, machine- or hand-stitch along all seam lines and inside circle at the stitched edge.

To finish

1. To create 1 long piece for the ruffle, cut and piece dark brown calico fabric together to create a strip 3½ × 112 inches.
2. With right sides facing and short edges even, join the brown strip to create a circle of fabric.
3. Divide the fabric into 4 equal parts and mark with pins.
4. Turn 1 long raw edge under ¼ inch

and press. Turn under another ¼ inch and stitch.
5. With right sides facing and raw edges aligned, pin ruffle strip to the pillow top, gathering the fabric between the pin markings to fit each pillow side. The ruffle is facing toward the center as you work. Baste around.
6. Cut backing piece from brown calico 15 × 15 inches. With right sides facing, pin backing to pillow top with ruffle between. Line up edges and pin ruffle down if necessary to keep it out of the way, temporarily, while joining front and back.
7. Stitch around 3 sides and 4 corners, leaving a ½-inch seam allowance. Clip corners and trim seam allowance.
8. Turn right side out and press. Insert pillow form and slip-stitch opening closed. Iron ruffle if needed.

SHOOFLY QUILT

This is a traditional 9-patch block quilt. It is a classic American patchwork design. To add to its basic appeal we've used a red, white, and blue color scheme, but you can use any fabric with light and dark backgrounds. If you're using cotton, which is often preferred by quilters, it's a good idea to wash the fabric before cutting it. If any shrinkage occurs, it won't affect the dimensions. Polyester is drip-dry and won't shrink. If the fabric used has any sizing in it, it's best to wash it before beginning the project. The finished project is 62 × 62 inches. This is a good size for a wall hanging or the top of a double bed. If you want to adjust the size for a twin bed, or a queen- or king-size bed, add or subtract more squares to one end or adjust the width of the border strips.

Materials

(all fabric is 45 inches wide)

1 yard solid blue fabric
1 yard white fabric
2 yards blue-and-white-printed fabric
4 yards red printed fabric
quilt batting 62 × 62 inches
5 skeins white embroidery floss
quilting needle
tracing paper
heavy paper or acetate for template
embroidery hoop

Directions

Trace the pattern piece and transfer to heavy paper for template (see page xiii). Seam allowance is included.

1. Trace pattern piece A and cut out 64 pieces from the solid blue fabric and 64 pieces from the white fabric.
2. Cut 64 blue-and-white-print squares $5\frac{1}{2} \times 5\frac{1}{2}$ inches (pattern piece B).
3. Cut 16 red squares $5\frac{1}{2} \times 5\frac{1}{2}$ inches (pattern piece C).
4. Cut red print for backing piece 64 × 64 inches. You might want to cut this piece after you have completed the top, but it is important to know that you will need the full yardage and to plan accordingly when cutting out the red print fabric squares.
5. With right sides facing and raw edges aligned, join all blue and white triangle pieces at the long edge to create 64 squares.

To make one block

Each block is made up of 9 squares. They are joined together according to Fig. 2.

1. With right sides facing and raw edges aligned, join an A square to a B square, followed by another A square. The A squares are all placed so that the white half of the fabric is in the outer corner. Open seams and press.
2. Next, join a B piece with a C piece, followed by another B piece. Open seams and press.

3. Make a third row of 3 patches by joining an A piece with a B piece, followed by another A piece. Remember to place the A squares with the white half of the fabric in the outer corners. Open seams and press.
4. With right sides facing and raw edges aligned, join all 3 rows to make the 9-patch square.
5. Make 16 blocks.

To assemble

1. With right sides facing and raw edges aligned, join 2 blocks at one side edge. Open seams and press.
2. Continue to make 4 rows of 4 blocks each in this way.
3. With right sides facing and raw edges aligned, join the first and second rows along one edge. Open seams and press.

Continue until you have stitched together 4 rows of 4 blocks each. Open all seams and press. (See Fig. 3.)

To quilt

Trace and transfer the heart pattern to each red square C. Trace the quilting pattern and transfer to the center of each white square. (See page xiii for transfer details.)

1. Pin the batting to the back of the quilt top so there is 1 inch all around. This extra batting extends beyond the fabric to account for the border that will be added later. Baste the fabric and batting loosely together.
2. Using 2 strands of embroidery floss, follow the drawn quilting lines with even backstitches.
3. When finished, remove all basting stitches.

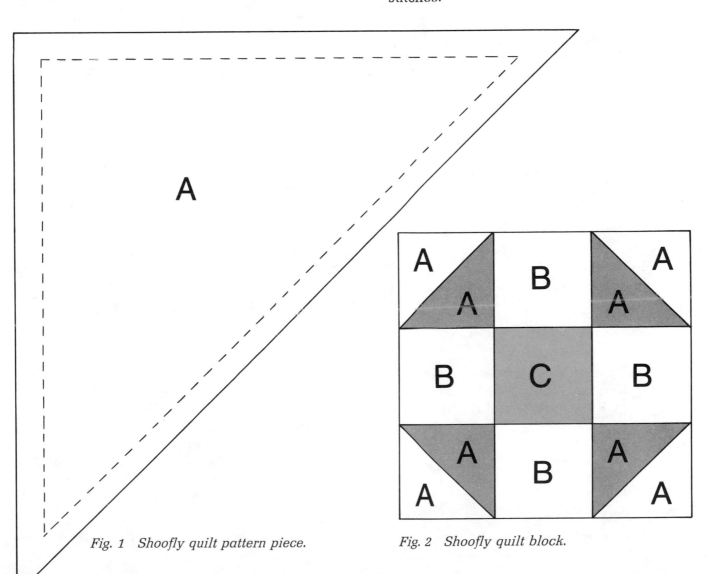

Fig. 1   Shoofly quilt pattern piece.

Fig. 2   Shoofly quilt block.

Fig. 3   Shoofly quilt assembly diagram.

4. You can quilt with running stitches inside all seam lines if you want more quilting on your fabric. It isn't necessary, however, for a pretty, finished quilt.

To finish

Place the quilted top over the wrong side of the backing fabric so that the backing extends 1½ inches beyond the top.

Turn backing edges forward ¼ inch and press all around. Fold turned edges forward to cover the raw edges of the quilt top and pin all around. Press. Stitch backing (which is now a 1-inch border around the quilt top) with a slip stitch or straight machine stitch all around.

Fig. 4   Shoofly quilting patterns.

EMBROIDERED TOTE BAG

All you need to make this pretty blue-and-red-quilted tote bag are small amounts of fabric, a little bit of muslin, and matching embroidery floss. Show off your needlework skills with this easy-to-make, easy-on-the-pocketbook project. The finished bag is 14¾ × 14¾ inches.

Materials

3/4 yard red printed 45-inch-wide fabric
1 piece muslin 8 × 8 inches
1/2 yard blue printed 45-inch-wide fabric
3/4 yard polyester batting
small piece of interfacing for straps
2 skeins blue embroidery floss to match the blue fabric
thread
needle
tracing paper
dressmaker's (carbon) paper
pencil

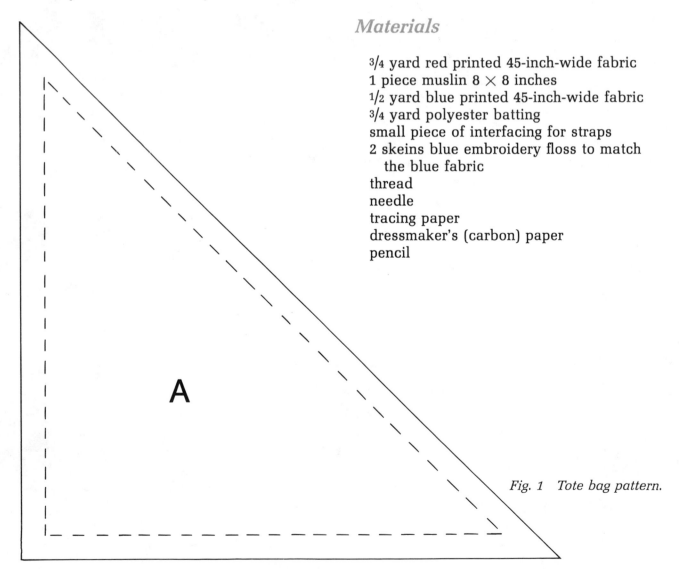

Fig. 1   Tote bag pattern.

Directions

Trace the triangle pattern piece A and use it to cut 4 from the red fabric, adding 1/4-inch seam allowance all around. Cut the following pieces:

RED PRINT:
2 pieces 2 × 11¼ inches (front border)
2 pieces 2 × 14 inches (front border)
1 piece 15¼ × 15¼ inches (back)
2 pieces 4 × 15¼ inches (sides)
1 piece 4 × 15¼ inches (bottom)

BLUE PRINT:
2 pieces 1 × 9¾ inches (inside border)
2 pieces 1 × 10¾ inches (inside border)
2 pieces 1½ × 14 inches (outer border)
2 pieces 1½ × 16 inches (outer border)
4 pieces 2½ × 15 inches (straps)
2 pieces 15¼ × 15¼ inches (front and back lining)
2 pieces 4 × 15¼ inches (lining sides)
1 piece 4 × 15¼ inches (bottom lining)

QUILT BATTING:
14½ × 14½ inches
7 × 7 inches

INTERFACING:
2 pieces 2 × 15 inches

Trace the quilting design and transfer to the center of the muslin square, using dressmaker's (carbon) paper. (See page xiii.)

1. Baste the small piece of batting to the muslin square and quilt the design using small backstitches made with 3 strands of embroidery floss.
2. With right sides facing and long edges aligned, stitch triangles to each side of the muslin square, using a 1/4-inch seam allowance. Open seams and press.
3. With right sides facing and edges aligned, stitch one blue inside border strip 1 × 9¾ inches to one side edge of the center square. Open seams and press.
4. Repeat on the opposite side.
5. Attach the 2 long inside border strips 1 × 10¾ inches to the remaining edges of the center square, leaving a 1/4-inch seam allowance. Open and press seams.

6. With right sides facing and edges aligned, attach a red 2 × 11¼-inch piece to one blue border edge, leaving a 1/4-inch seam allowance. Open seams and press. Repeat on the opposite side.
7. Sew remaining red strips 2 × 14 inches to the top and bottom edges as above. Open seams and press.

Outside blue border
1. With right sides facing and raw edges aligned, sew the 2 blue strips 1½ × 14 inches to opposite sides of the front red border.
2. Repeat with the remaining blue border strips 1½ × 16 inches. Open seams and press.

Quilting
1. Pin the 14½ × 14½ piece of batting to the back of the bag front.
2. Using 3 strands of blue embroidery floss, take small backstitches around the edges of each red triangle just inside the seam line.

To assemble bag
1. With right sides facing and edges aligned, stitch sides of the bag front. Open seams and press.
2. Attach the bottom strip 4 × 15¼ inches in the same way to the bottom edge of the bag front.
3. With right sides facing, join the short side edges to the short edges of the bottom strip. This completes the front, side, and bottom of the bag.
4. With right sides facing, attach back red panel to sides and bottom section of the bag.
5. Assemble lining pieces in the same way as for outer bag.

Straps
1. Place interfacing strip on the wrong side of one strap piece. Turn under 1/4-inch

Fig. 2   Quilting design for tote bag.

seam allowance of interfacing and fabric to wrong side and press.

2. Turn under 1/4-inch seam allowance to wrong side on second strap piece and press. Pin to first strap piece with wrong sides facing and the interfacing between.

3. Topstitch close to the edge along both long edges. Topstitch again 1/4 inch from the first stitching. Repeat for second strap.

4. Measure 3 1/4 inches from each front side seam. Mark with a pin for the placement of the strap ends on the inside of the bag. Repeat on the back with the second strap.

Assembled tote bag.

To finish

1. With wrong sides facing, slip the lining inside the finished bag. Line up side seams and pin in position.
2. Turn top raw edges of the lining and the outer bag to the inside 1/2 inch and press.
3. Slip the strap ends between lining and outer fabric where previously marked and pin in position.
4. Topstitch 1/4 inch from edge all around top of the bag through outer bag, lining, and straps.
5. Tack the lining at the four bottom corners. Remove all pins and press finished bag.

EYEGLASS CASE

The finished size of this eyeglass case is $3^1/2 \times 7$ inches, which is an ample size to hold any glasses, even oversized sunglasses.

This is a nice beginner's project that ends up looking as if it were much more difficult. The quilting is confined to the center panel which is embroidered with a flower and initials. The embroidery quilts and adds decoration. The inside is lined with a contrasting red printed calico to match the tote on page 42.

Materials

10 × 15 inches blue-and-white-printed fabric

2¹/₂ × 6 inches unbleached muslin
10 × 15 inches red printed fabric for lining
thin quilt batting
1 skein blue embroidery floss
needle
tracing paper
dressmaker's (carbon) paper

Directions

1. From the blue fabric, cut 1 piece $4 \times 7^1/2$ inches for the back.
2. From the remaining blue fabric, cut 2 strips $1^1/2 \times 7^1/2$ inches. Cut 2 pieces $1^1/2 \times 2$ inches.

Fig. 1 Eyeglass case alphabet.

46

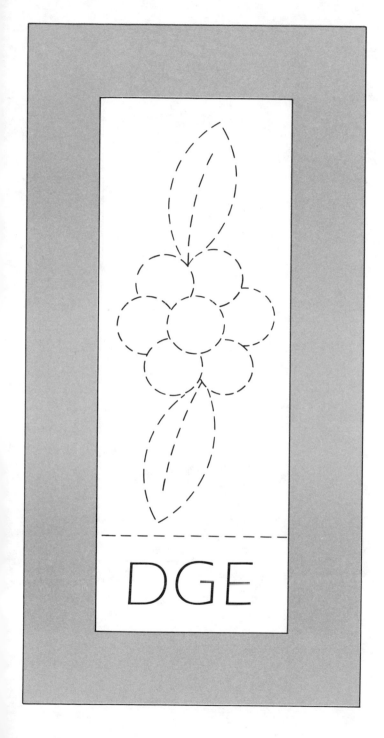

Fig. 2   Eyeglass case pattern, quilting design, and layout.

Fig. 3   Alternate quilting design for eyeglass case.

3. Cut 2 red pieces 3$\frac{1}{2}$ × 7$\frac{1}{2}$ inches for the lining.
4. Cut 2 pieces of batting 3 × 6$\frac{1}{2}$ inches.
5. With right sides facing and raw edges aligned, join the short blue strips 1$\frac{1}{2}$ × 2 inches to each short end of the muslin, leaving a $\frac{1}{4}$-inch seam allowance. Open seams and press.
6. Next, attach the 2 long blue strips 1$\frac{1}{2}$ × 7$\frac{1}{2}$ inches to each side edge of the muslin in the same way.

To quilt

Trace the design and appropriate initials from the book. Place a piece of carbon paper on the center panel of muslin with the tracing on top. Retrace over the design to transfer it. Center the initials at the bottom edge of the muslin and transfer them in the same way.

1. Pin 1 piece of batting to the back of the entire front piece. The batting will be slightly smaller all around.
2. Using 3 strands of embroidery floss, follow your design outlines using a small, even backstitch.
3. Stitch around the muslin panel in the same way, approximately 1/8 inch outside the seam line on the blue fabric.
4. Topstitch around the outside edge of the entire fabric 1/2 inch in from the raw edges.

To finish

1. Pin the remaining piece of batting to the wrong side of the blue, back fabric piece.
2. With right sides facing and raw edges aligned, stitch the back piece to the front with a 1/4-inch seam allowance and leaving the top edge open. Turn right side out and press.
3. With right sides facing and raw edges aligned, stitch the 2 lining pieces together with a 1/4-inch seam allowance and leaving the top edge open. *Do not turn right side out.* Press.
4. Slip the lining inside the outside case and adjust so that it fits comfortably.
5. Turn the top raw edges of the outside case and the lining 1/4 inch to the inside (between outside and lining) and press. Slip-stitch all around to finish.

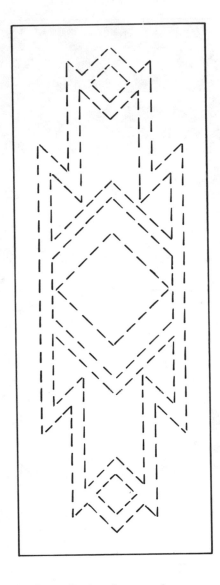

Fig. 4 *Quilting design for eyeglass case without monogram.*

48

PLATE 7 Piggy Placemat, Piggy Bib

PLATE 8 Ducky Placemat, Ducky Bib

PLATE 9 Piggy Wallhanging, Piggy Pillow

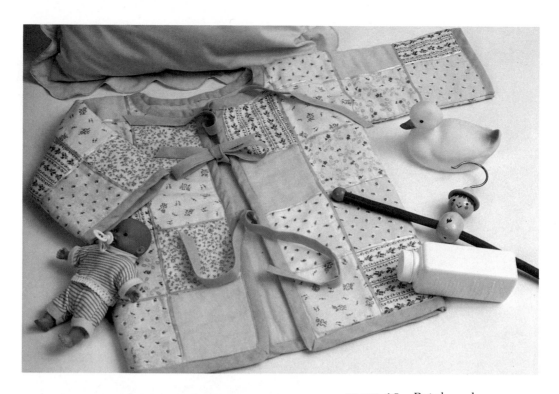

PLATE 10 Patchwork
Flannel Baby Jacket

PLATE 11 Pinwheel Crib
Quilt, Pinwheel Crib Pillows

PLATE 12 · Teddy Bear Quilt

Book Two

First Steps in Quilting for Baby

PIGGY PLACE MAT

Won't your child enjoy sitting down to a meal served on his or her own little piggy place mat? You can make several to give as gifts. Once you get started, it's easy to cut and stitch the appliqués by hand or machine. The finished size is 11½ × 15½ inches.

Materials

1/3 yard 45-inch-wide pink-and-white-
   striped fabric
scraps of 3 different pink prints
polyester batting

pink thread
needle
tracing paper
heavy paper for template

Directions

1. Cut 2 pieces of fabric 12 × 16 inches.
2. Trace the pig pattern and transfer to heavy paper to make a template (see pages x and xiii).
3. Place the template on each of the 3 different fabric scraps and draw around the shape.

Fig. 1   Piggy place mat layout.

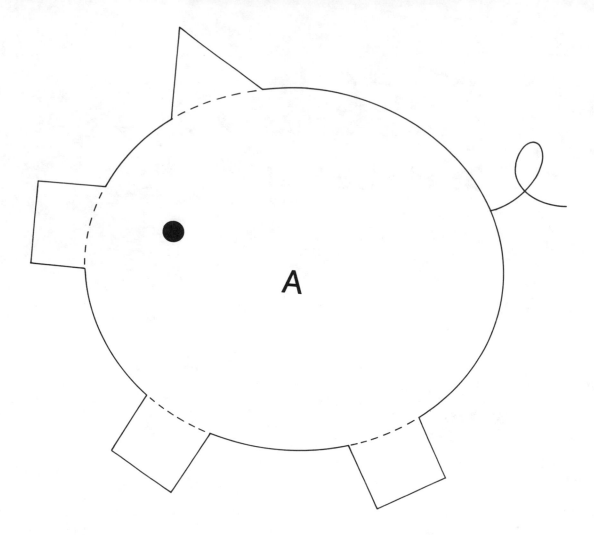

To appliqué

By hand: Cut each appliqué with a ³/₈-inch seam allowance.

1. Place one pig appliqué fabric face down on an ironing board. Place the template on the back of the fabric and clip in around the seam allowance.
2. Using a medium-hot iron, press the raw edges over the edge of the template all around. Remove the template and press down on the back of the fabric. Repeat on the other 2 appliqués.
3. Pin each appliqué in position on the front of the fabric top piece, right side up and with all edges turned under.
4. With right side up, baste the top fabric to the piece of batting. Stitch the appliqués to the fabric and batting with a blind stitch around all edges.
5. To quilt the appliqués, take small running stitches around the outside edge of each appliqué. (See page xviii for quilting details.)

Fig. 2   Piggy place mat appliqué pattern.

By machine: Cut the appliqué fabric as marked, with no seam allowance.

1. Place the top piece of the place mat over the batting and baste around the edges.
2. Pin the pig appliqués in position on the top of the fabric (see diagram). Using a narrow zigzag stitch and matching thread, stitch around the edges of each appliqué.

To finish

1. With right sides facing and raw edges aligned, pin backing fabric to appliquéd top piece.
2. Leaving a ¹/₄-inch seam allowance, stitch around 3 sides and 4 corners, leaving 6 inches open for turning.
3. Trim the corners and turn right side out. Press. Stitch opening closed with a slip stitch.

4

DUCKY PLACE MAT

Brighten up your child's eating area with a pretty blue place mat with 3 little ducks all in a row. It's easy to stitch these appliqués with a zigzag attachment on your sewing machine. And since they're easy and quick to make, you might consider this item for bazaar sales. The finished size is 11½ × 15½ inches.

Materials

1/3 yard 45-inch-wide blue-and-white-printed fabric
scraps of white fabric
scraps of yellow fabric
polyester batting
white and yellow thread
needle
tracing paper
heavy paper for template

Directions

1. Cut 2 pieces of blue fabric 12 × 16 inches.
2. Trace the duck elements for body, bill, and feet and transfer them to heavy paper to make templates (see pages x and xiii).
3. Place the template for each body on white fabric and draw around each. You will need 1 of pattern A shape and 2 of pattern B (for pattern B, see plans for Ducky bib).
4. Draw around the little triangles and bill pieces for each duck on bright yellow fabric.

To appliqué

If you do not have a zigzag attachment on your sewing machine, cut each appliqué

Fig. 1   Ducky place mat patterns.

5

Fig. 2 Ducky place mat layout.

piece large enough to turn the raw edges under neatly. (See page xvi for hand appliqué.)

1. Cut the appliqué fabric pieces as marked, with no seam allowance.
2. Place one blue rectangle right side up on the batting and baste around 1/4 inch from the raw edge.
3. Pin each duck piece in position on the place mat as indicated on the diagram.
4. Using a narrow zigzag stitch and matching thread, stitch around the edges of the appliqués.
5. If desired, add stitches at random for rain and stitch a fat cloud in one corner using a backstitch or running stitch.

To finish

1. Place the backing piece of fabric right side down over the appliquéd front. Align edges and pin together.
2. Leaving a 1/4-inch seam allowance, stitch around 3 sides and 4 corners, leaving 6 inches open for turning.
3. Trim the corners and turn right side out. Press. Stitch the opening closed with a slip stitch.

DUCKY BIB

Two little ducks on a bright blue bib will delight any baby and is the perfect gift for a toddler. The simple appliqués are machine-stitched with a zigzag attachment all around in matching thread colors. If you do not have such an attachment, it will be necessary to cut larger appliqué pieces so you have enough material all around for turning the edges neatly. (See page xvi for hand appliqué.)

Directions

1. Trace and enlarge the outline pattern for the bib (see page xiii). Pin the pattern to the 2 pieces of 12 × 14-inch blue fabric.
2. Cut out with a 1/4-inch seam allowance all around.
3. Use the same pattern to cut a piece of polyester batting the same size without the seam allowance.

Materials

2 pieces bright blue fabric
   12 × 14 inches
scrap of white fabric
scrap of bright yellow fabric
polyester batting
yellow and white thread
2¼ yards extra-wide double-fold yellow
   bias tape
needle
tracing paper
heavy paper or template

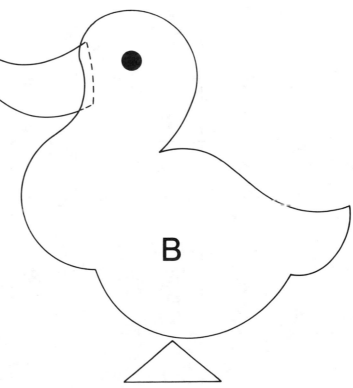

Fig. 1 Ducky bib appliqué patterns.

7

Each square equals 1″

Fig. 2 Bib pattern.

4. Trace the elements of the duck pattern and make templates on heavy paper for body, bill, and feet (see pages xi and xiii).
5. Draw around the body templates A and B on the white fabric. Draw around the little triangle and bill pieces for each duck on bright yellow fabric.

To appliqué

These appliqué pieces are quite small and difficult to do by hand. A zigzag attachment on your sewing machine is necessary to attach them.

1. Cut the appliqué fabric pieces as marked, with no seam allowance.
2. Place the bib front right side up on the batting and baste around 1/4 inch from the raw edge.
3. Pin each duck piece in position on the bib front as indicated in the diagram.
4. Using a narrow zigzag stitch and matching thread, stitch around the edges of the appliqués.

To finish

1. Place the backing fabric right side down on the table. Place the bib front and batting over the fabric and pin together.
2. Beginning at one neck edge, pin the bias binding around the raw outer edge of all 3 layers.
3. Leaving 8 inches at each end for ties, pin the bias binding around the neck opening. Stitch around all binding.
4. Overlap the open tie edges and stitch together.

PIGGY BIB

It's easy to create a pretty and practical bib for your baby. The pig appliqué is made from one printed piece of fabric and outlined in a zigzag stitch. If you don't have this attachment on your sewing machine, you can make an appliqué by hand. Make several to sell at your next bazaar. They are always popular.

Materials

2 pieces pink and white fabric 12 × 14 inches
scrap of pink printed fabric
polyester batting
pink thread
2¼ yards extra-wide double-fold bias tape
needle
tracing paper
heavy paper for template

Directions

1. Trace and enlarge the outline pattern for the bib (see pages xi and xiii). Pin the pattern to the 2 pieces of 12 × 14-inch pink and white fabric.
2. Cut out with a ¼-inch seam allowance all around.
3. Use the same pattern to cut a piece of polyester batting the same size without the seam allowance.
4. Trace the pig pattern and make a template on heavy paper (see pages x and xiii).
5. Draw around the template on the front of the pink printed fabric scrap. This will become the appliqué on the bib front.

To appliqué

By hand: Cut the appliqué fabric with a ⅜-inch seam allowance.

1. Place the pig fabric right side down on an ironing board. Place the template on the back of the fabric and clip in around the seam allowance.
2. Using a medium-hot iron, press the raw edges over the edge of the template all around. Remove the template and press down on the back of the fabric.
3. Pin the appliqué in position on the front of the bib right side up and all edges turned under.
4. With right side up, baste the bib front to the piece of batting. Take small blind stitches around the appliqué, securing it to the fabric and batting.
5. *To quilt the appliqué:* take small running stitches around the outside edge of the appliqué. (See page xviii for more quilting details.)

By machine: Cut the appliqué fabric as marked, with no seam allowance.

1. Place the bib front right side up on the

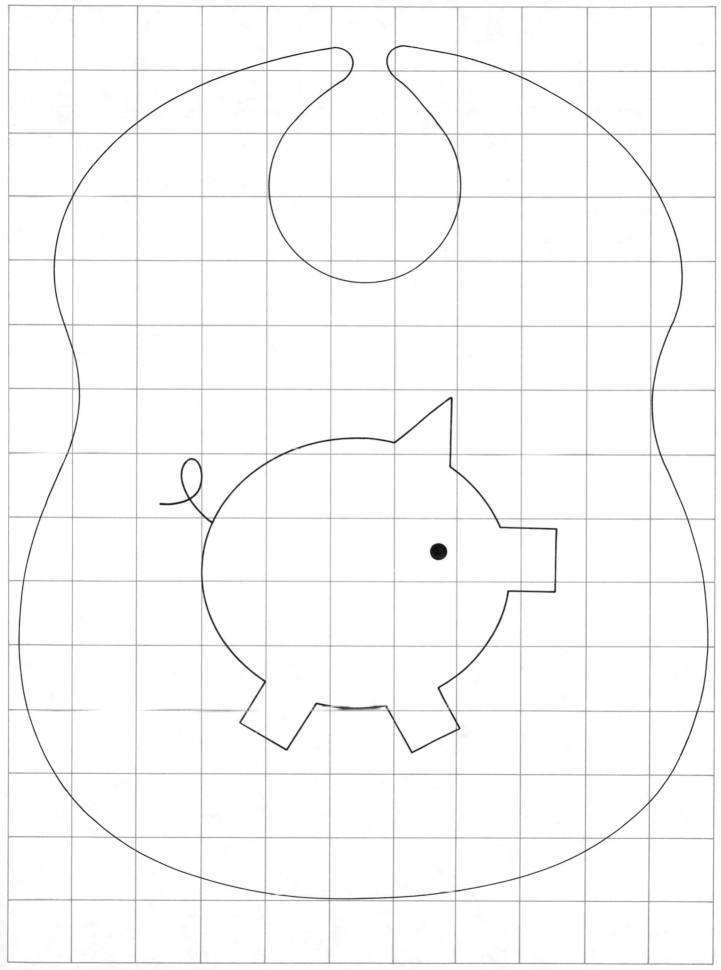

Each square equals 1″

Fig. 1   Piggy appliqué pattern.

batting and baste around 1/4 inch from raw edge.

2. Center and pin the pig appliqué in position on the bib front. Using a narrow zig-zag stitch and matching thread, stitch around the edges of the appliqué.

To finish

1. Place the backing fabric right side down on table. Top with the bib front and batting. Pin together.
2. Beginning at one neck edge, pin the bias binding around the raw, outer edge of all 3 layers.
3. Leaving 8 inches at each end for ties, pin the bias binding around the neck opening. Stitch around all binding.
4. Overlap the open tie edges and stitch together.

PIGGY WALL HANGING

One appliqué of a fat, little pig is used to create a wall hanging of 9 pigs made from 3 different pink fabrics. Small, overall prints are best for this project and, if you use scraps, you will need a 5-inch-square piece for each appliqué.

Each appliqué is one piece. The appliqués should be applied with a zigzag stitch on the machine. For these, this is the only way to make perfect appliqués, since it would be too difficult to turn all the edges by hand on such small appliqués and make each identical to the others.

The finished project is 21×23 inches.

Materials

1/4 yard of 3 different pink printed fabrics
1 strip of pink printed fabric 5 × 22 inches

1 strip of solid pink fabric 5 × 25 inches
1/2 yard white fabric, 45 inches wide
backing material 21½ × 23½ inches (can be muslin)
thin quilt batting
pink and white thread
small amounts of black and pink embroidery floss
tracing paper
heavy paper for template
dressmaker's (carbon) paper
pencil and ruler

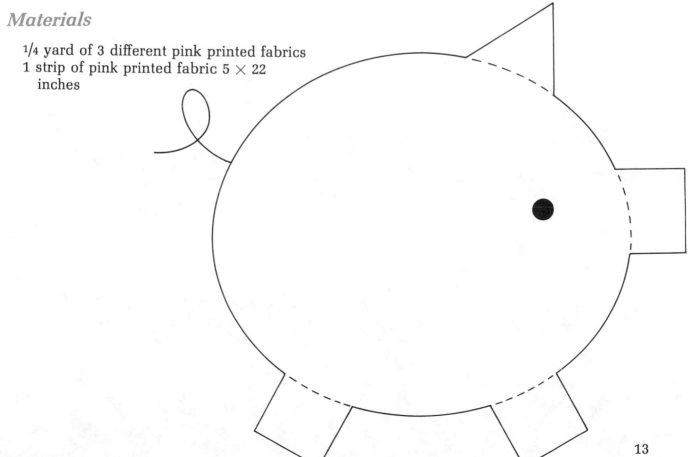

This little piggy went to market

Piggy pillow pattern.

14

Fig. 2 Piggy wall hanging layout.

Directions

Trace and transfer the pig pattern to heavy paper for template (see page xiii).

1. Without adding any seam allowance, cut 3 pigs from each of 3 different pink fabrics.
2. Cut white fabric 18 × 21 inches.
3. Measure 3 inches up from the bottom edge of the white fabric and, using a ruler and light pencil, draw a line across the fabric.
4. Rule off the remaining fabric into 3 rows of 6-inch squares.
5. From the strip of pink printed fabric 5 × 22 inches, cut 2 strips 1¼ × 18 inches and 2 strips 1¼ × 22 inches.
6. With right sides facing and edges aligned, stitch one of these short pink printed strips to the top of the white fabric. Open seams and press. Repeat on the bottom edge.
7. From the solid pink fabric strip 5 × 25 inches, cut 2 strips 1¼ × 19 inches and 2 strips 1¼ × 24 inches.
8. With right sides facing and edges aligned, join one of these short solid strips to the top and bottom of the printed border. Open seams and press.
9. Repeat on the side edges with the larger strips. The white fabric now has a 1-inch printed inside border and a 1-inch solid outside border all around.

To appliqué
1. Cut a piece of thin batting ¼ inch smaller all around than the white background fabric piece and pin to the back.
2. Center each pig shape on a ruled off square. (See color plate for placement.) The pigs in the top row of squares should all face to the left. In the second row all the pigs face to the right and those in the last row face left again. Pin each one in place.
3. Using white thread, stitch along the pencil lines dividing the fabric into squares.
4. Using a narrow zigzag stitch and pink thread, stitch around the outline of the appliqué for each pig.
5. Using a straight stitch, sew along the seam lines of the borders.

To embroider
1. Using dressmaker's (carbon) paper and a tracing of the pig's tail, transfer the outline to each appliqué in position as shown. (See page xiii for transfer details.)
2. Make a mark to indicate where each eye will be placed (approximately 1½ inches from the middle of the end of the snout).
3. Trace the words "This little piggy went to market" on one line. Tape the tracing in position on the wall hanging. Slip a piece of carbon paper under the tracing.
4. Retrace the words and remove the paper and carbon.
5. Using 2 strands of pink embroidery floss, take small backstitches along the pencil lines for the pigs' tails and the words at the bottom of the hanging.
6. Using 3 strands of black floss, make a satin stitch for each eye. (See page xix for stitch guide.)

To finish
Place backing piece right side down over the appliquéd fabric and stitch around the raw edges with ¼-inch seam allowance, leaving 8 inches open on the top. Clip off the corners and turn right side out. Press all around. Close opening with a slip stitch.

To hang
This wall hanging is small and light and therefore easy to hang. Unlike a heavy quilt there is no special method. One of the easiest ways to attach it to a wall area is with small Velcro tabs. Found in notions and hardware stores, a small package provides all the material and information needed to do the job.

PIGGY PILLOW

Save scraps of pink solid and printed fabric for a darling little pig pillow to place in the corner of a crib or on a teenager's dresser. It is easy to make and will cost next to nothing. The quilting can be done by hand or on the machine. The tail is made from a pipe cleaner, but if this is to be a baby item, substitute a piece of ribbon or fabric secured with carpet thread.

Materials

scraps of solid pink fabric
scraps of pink and white flower print
scraps of pink print
thin quilt batting
Poly-Fil® stuffing
pink thread
small amount of black embroidery floss for eye
embroidery needle
tracing paper

Directions

Enlarge the outline of the pig shape and each pattern piece (see page xiii). Use the tracings as your pattern pieces and add 1/4 inch to each side for seam allowance. Cut the following pieces:

From solid pink fabric: piece 1 and 5

From floral print: piece 2, 6 and 7
From pink print: piece 3, 4 and 8

Use the pig pattern to cut a solid piece from one fabric color for the backing.

Cut 1 piece of batting the same size as the pattern. Do not add seam allowance.

To assemble

1. With right sides facing and edges aligned, stitch piece 1 to piece 2, as indicated on the diagram. Press seams open.
2. Continue in this way by joining piece 3 to 2.
3. Next, join piece 4 to 5. Open seams and press.
4. Join piece 6 to 5. You now have 2 strips of 3 pieces each.
5. With right sides facing and raw edges aligned, join piece 7 to piece 8.
6. With right sides facing and raw edges aligned, join strip 1–2–3 to strip 4–5–6. Open seams and press.
7. Attach strip 7–8 to 4–5–6 as shown. Open seams and press. You now have a patchwork square.
8. Using the pig pattern, pin to the patchwork fabric and cut out with a 1/4-inch seam allowance added.

To quilt

1. Pin the pig patchwork top to the batting.
2. Using pink thread, machine-stitch 1/8 inch inside each seam line.
3. Stitch around outline 1/4 inch from the outside edge.

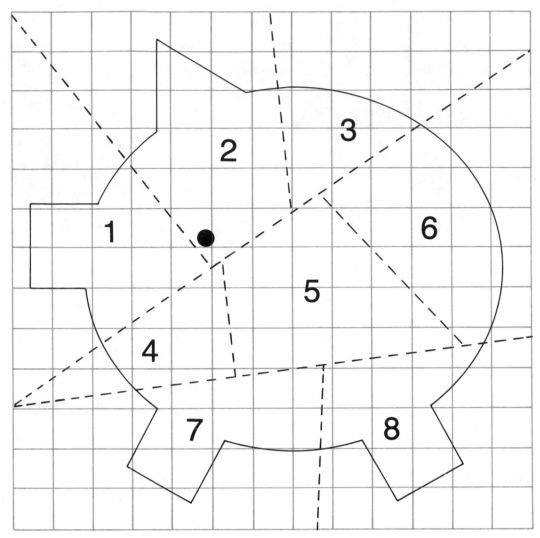

Each square equals 1″

Fig. 1   Piggy pattern pieces.

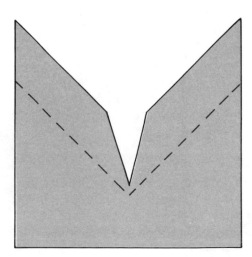

Fig. 3   Clip off all corner pieces.

Fig. 2   Clip in at each corner.

To finish

1. With right sides facing, pin front and back pieces together and stitch around the edge, leaving approximately 4 inches open where the tail will be placed.
2. Clip around the curved edges to the stitch line. Clip in at each corner where the tail, snout, and feet meet the body. Clip off all corner pieces.
3. Turn right side out and press.
4. Stuff with Poly-Fil®. To push stuffing into corners use a blunt object such as a crochet hook or the end of an artist's brush.
5. Cut a 2-inch piece of pink yarn, pipe cleaner, or narrow piece of felt for the tail. Insert between the fabric pieces at the opening and pin.
6. Slip-stitch opening closed, securing the tail with extra stitches. You might want to use carpet thread if the pillow will be placed in a baby's crib.

PATCHWORK FLANNEL BABY JACKET

Make a soft, warm, kimono-style jacket for a small child. The fabric choices are limitless. I've used a variety of soft, pastel, flannel scraps to make a patchwork pattern. The scraps are cut into squares, stitched together with a thin ribbon between each square, and lightly quilted. The edges are finished with bias binding. The finished size is 16 × 13½ inches.

Materials

A variety of flannel scraps or 3/4 yard fabric
1/2 yard flannel for lining
1/2 yard thin quilt batting
4 yards 1/8-inch satin ribbon
1 package 1/2-inch-wide double-fold bias binding
thread color to match satin ribbon

Directions

1. Cut 40 scrap flannel pieces into 4-inch squares.
2. Cut 8 squares for shoulder area, 4 × 5 inches.
3. Refer to diagram 1. With right sides facing and raw edges aligned, join 2 of the 40 squares along one side, leaving a 1/4-inch seam allowance. Open seams and press.
4. Make 3 more sets of 2 squares each in this way.
5. With right sides facing and raw edges aligned, join all squares together so you have 4 rows of 2. Repeat for opposite side of front of jacket.
6. Continue to join all squares as indicated on the diagram, making sure to place the 8 larger squares across the middle of the arm and neck section.
7. You now have a patchwork cross. Place this on your lining fabric and cut out the entire shape. Cut a 14-inch slit up the middle front of the lining.
8. Cut an oval from both fabrics for neck opening as indicated on the diagram.

To quilt

1. Remove the patchwork top piece and use this as a pattern to cut a batting piece. Trim batting slightly all around. Pin the batting piece to the back of the flannel top.
2. Pin lengths of ribbon over all seam lines to create a grid, outlining all patchwork squares.
3. Machine-stitch over the ribbon with matching thread color.

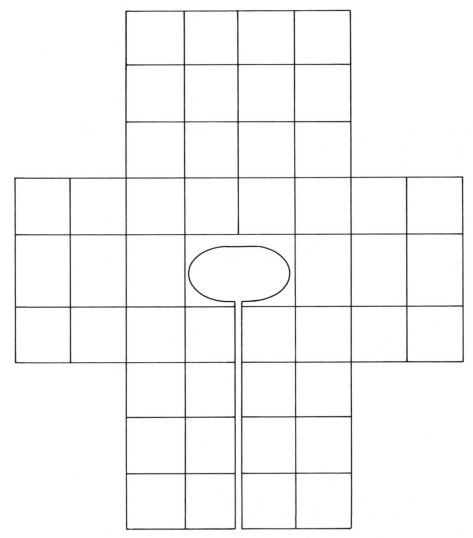

Fig. 1   Patchwork flannel baby jacket layout.

To finish

1. With right sides facing and raw edges aligned, stitch the back side seams to the front side seams, continuing along the sleeve and underarms. Turn right side out and press.
2. Repeat for lining but do not turn. Press.
3. Slip lining inside top piece and adjust so sleeve edges and front opening line up. Pin together along all outside edges.
4. Bind all edges with bias binding. Bind neck opening.
5. Cut 6 pieces of binding 10 inches long and stitch one on each side of neck opening for ties. Position the next 2 ties 3 inches from the first and stitch to the inside edge of front opening. Repeat with the last set of ties.

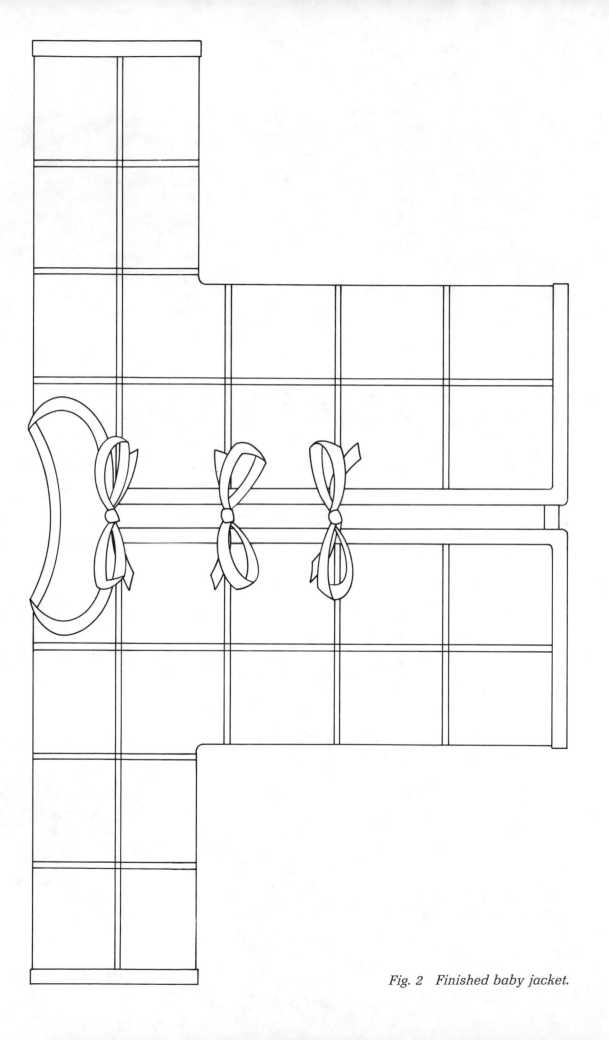

Fig. 2 Finished baby jacket.

PINWHEEL CRIB QUILT

Choose soft, pastel colors for a pretty baby quilt. This one is easy to make as only one template is used to make all the pattern pieces. The fabric used here is slightly shiny, like chintz. If you use fabric like this, or one that has sizing in it (which gives it a sheen and feels slightly stiff), prewash the fabric with softener before beginning. This will make it easier to quilt by hand and will ensure against shrinkage after the project is finished. The finished size is 36 × 52 inches.

Materials

3/4 yard light blue printed fabric
3/4 yard light green printed fabric
2 1/2 yards yellow fabric
1 1/2 yards peach fabric
quilt batting
embroidery floss to match fabric colors
needle
tracing paper
heavy paper for template

Directions

Trace the pattern piece A, which includes a 1/4-inch seam allowance. This pattern represents half the piece needed. To make it full size, transfer the design to heavy paper and then turn it over on the fold (the broken line) and trace the other half, making one large triangle shape. Or you can transfer the half pattern to heavy paper for a template (see page xiii). Fold the fabric in half so you have a double layer. Place the template on the fold line to cut. Either of these methods eliminate the need for enlarging a pattern piece that is too large to fit, full-size, on a book page. Use the template to cut the following from each fabric:

12 pieces light blue
12 pieces light green
24 pieces yellow

Cut sash and border strips as follows:

peach—cut 3 strips 3 1/2 × 14 1/2 inches
cut 4 strips 3 1/2 × 31 1/2 inches
cut 2 strips 3 1/2 × 54 1/2 inches

Cut a piece of batting 35 1/2 × 51 1/2 inches. Cut backing piece from yellow fabric 36 1/2 × 52 1/2 inches.

To make one block
1. With right sides facing and raw edges aligned, join a yellow piece with a blue piece along the long edge (see the diagram). Open seams and press.
2. Repeat 3 more times to make 4 squares.
3. Refer to the diagram to join squares to complete the quilt block.

Joining blocks
1. With right sides facing and raw edges aligned, stitch one short peach sash 3 1/2 × 14 1/2 inches to the right side edge of one quilt block, using a 1/4-inch seam allowance. Open seams and press.

2. Join the next block to the long, raw edge of the sash to make a row of 2 blocks separated by the sash strip. Open seams and press.
3. Repeat to make 2 more rows.
4. With right sides facing and raw edges aligned, pin one of the 4 long sashes 3½ × 31½ inches to the bottom edges of the first row of blocks.
5. Stitch together, open seams, and press.
6. Repeat to join all block rows.
7. Stitch the 2 remaining border strips in the same way along the top and bottom edges of the quilt.
8. Attach the remaining long border strips 3½ × 54½ inches to each side of the quilt in the same way.

To quilt
1. Pin the top of the quilt to the batting, which has been cut slightly smaller all around to avoid being in the seam allowance.
2. Using 2 strands of embroidery floss in the color of each fabric, take running stitches or backstitches ⅛ inch inside each seam line. You can also use a machine to do this.

To finish
With right sides facing and raw edges aligned, stitch around 3 sides and 4 corners, leaving approximately 12 inches open across the top for turning. Clip corners and turn right side out. Press and slip-stitch opening closed.

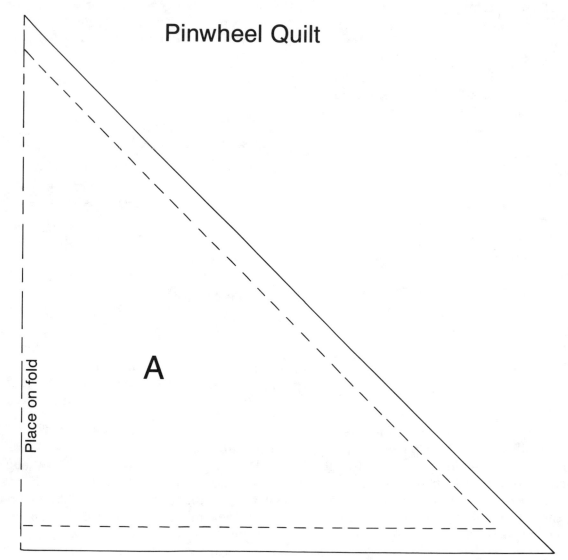

Pinwheel Quilt

Place on fold

A

Fig. 1 Pinwheel crib quilt pattern.

Fig. 2   Pinwheel crib quilt layout.

PINWHEEL CRIB PILLOWS

A pinwheel pillow is the perfect small quilting project. This design and fabric match the pinwheel quilt, and each pillow uses a slightly different color combination of the same fabric.

Each pillow is finished with a matching piping and measures 12 × 12 inches. This is a standard pillow size for which you can buy a form. However, if you stuff the finished pillow with Poly-Fil®, you can make it slightly smaller in order to use only 1/3 yard of fabric for the backing, rather than 1/2 yard. Directions are given for a 12-inch pillow, with a 1/4-inch seam allowance for all sewing.

Materials
(for 2 pillows)

1/2 yard peach fabric
1/2 yard blue fabric
1/3 yard green fabric
1/3 yard yellow fabric
quilting batting
12 × 12 inch pillow form or Poly-Fil®
   stuffing
1 yard cording
thread in color of fabric
needle
tracing paper
heavy paper for templates

Directions

Trace and transfer pattern pieces A and B to heavy paper to make templates (see page xiii). A 1/4-inch seam allowance is included.

PILLOW 1: Using the templates, cut the fabric in the following way:

4 green pieces for A
4 yellow pieces for B
4 peach pieces for B

For the border cut 2 yellow strips 11/2 × 101/2 inches and 2 strips 11/2 × 121/2 inches.
Cut backing piece 121/2 × 121/2 inches from the peach fabric.

To assemble
1. With right sides facing and raw edges aligned, sew a yellow B piece to a peach B piece along one edge (see Fig. 2). Open seams and press. You now have a large triangle.
2. Repeat with remaining yellow and peach B pieces.
3. With right sides facing and long edges aligned, stitch all yellow/peach triangles to each green triangle A piece. Open seams and press.
4. Refer to the diagram and join all 4 squares, making a small pinwheel in the center of the pillow top. Open seams and press.

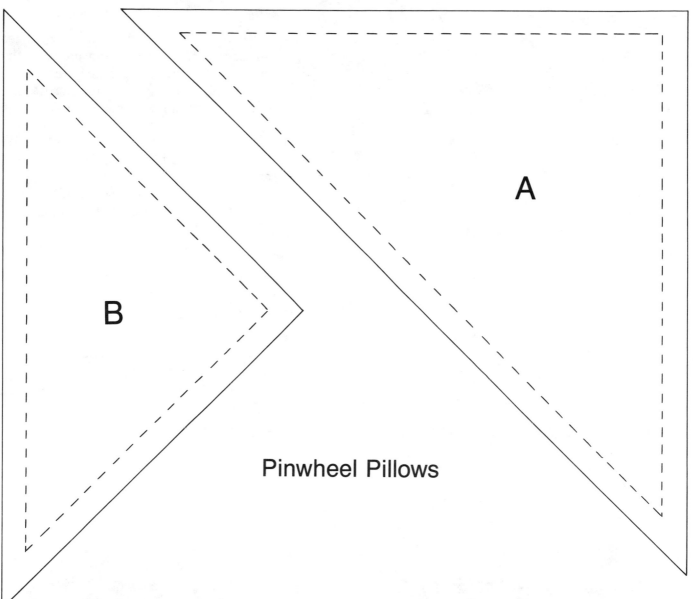

A

B

Pinwheel Pillows

Fig. 1 Pinwheel pillow patterns.

5. Next, add the borders in the following way. With right sides facing and raw edges aligned, attach a short $1^1/_2 \times 10^1/_2$-inch strip to one edge of the block. Stitch across. Open and press seams. Repeat on the opposite side.

6. Join the long strips in the same way to complete the pillow top.

To quilt

1. Cut quilt batting $11^1/_2 \times 11^1/_2$ inches and pin to the back of the fabric.

2. Using 1 strand of embroidery floss or 2 strands of thread, sew along all seam lines to quilt with a running stitch.

To finish

Cut a strip of fabric $1^1/_2 \times 50$ inches long for the piping. This piece can be made by stitching together shorter pieces. You can use any one of the fabric colors.

1. Beginning $1/_2$ inch from the end of the fabric, encase the cording of the fabric, using a zipper foot on your machine.

2. With right sides facing and raw edges aligned, pin the piping around the edge of the pillow top, overlapping the ends. Stitch around as close to cording as possible.

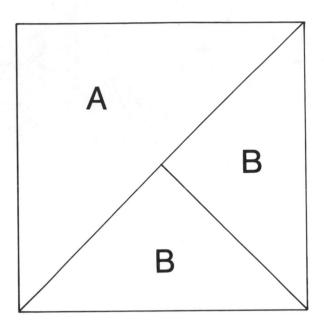

Fig. 2   Pinwheel pillow pattern for one square.

3. With right sides facing and raw edges aligned, stitch the backing piece to the pillow top, using the piping stitches as a guide and leaving 8 inches across one edge open. Trim seams and clip corners. Turn right side out and press.
4. Insert pillow form or fill firmly with stuffing. Use a blunt object such as the eraser end of a pencil or a crochet hook to get stuffing into the corners.
5. Slip-stitch opening closed.

PILLOW 2: Using the templates, cut fabric pieces for the following patterns:

4 blue pieces for A
4 yellow pieces for B
4 peach pieces for B

For the border cut 2 peach strips $1\frac{1}{2} \times 10\frac{1}{2}$ inches and 2 strips $1\frac{1}{2} \times 12\frac{1}{2}$ inches.

Cut backing piece $12\frac{1}{2} \times 12\frac{1}{2}$ inches from blue fabric.

Follow the directions for pillow 1.

Pillow #1

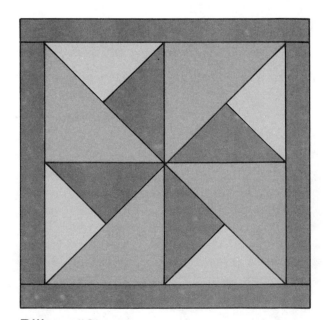

Pillow #2

Fig. 3   Pinwheel pillow layout.

TEDDY BEAR QUILT

A crib quilt is an easy project as it is a manageable size for machine appliqué.

The pattern pieces such as the bear's body, pants, and balloons are large shapes that are easily applied to the background fabric. If you have a zigzag attachment on your sewing machine, use this technique. If not, the shapes can be appliquéd by hand without difficulty. Both methods are provided in the directions.

The finished size is 38 × 54 inches. This is ample for most cribs. However, if you want to make yours larger, or make the quilt to fit a twin bed, simply increase the width of the borders to accommodate the larger bed size. In this way, you can adjust the size without changing the design.

Materials

6 × 8-inch fabric pieces in the following colors: red, orange, blue, purple, and green
1/4 yard light brown fabric
12 × 16-inch piece of red fabric
scraps of white fabric
small piece of black felt
1 yard 45-inch-wide yellow gingham fabric
1 1/2 yards 45-inch-wide brown calico
38 × 54-inch piece of cotton batting
1 skein black embroidery floss
embroidery needle
tracing paper
heavy paper for template
dressmaker's (carbon) paper
white glue

Directions

Begin by enlarging all pattern pieces (see page xiii). The bear shape will be cut as one large piece from the brown calico fabric, rather than its arms, legs, and head cut separately. Therefore, enlarge this shape and then enlarge the pants separately as another pattern piece to be placed over the bear's body.

1. Trace each enlarged pattern piece and cut as follows with no seam allowance for zigzag appliqué (for hand appliqué, add 3/8-inch seam allowance):
   each balloon shape from 1 of the 6 × 8-inch fabric pieces
   the inner ears, paws, feet pads, and center face pieces from light brown fabric
2. From the white fabric, cut the pants' button and 2 circles for the eyes.
3. Using a small button as a template, draw a circle on plain paper for each buttonhole and the centers of the eyes. Use these as patterns to cut each circle from black felt.

To appliqué

Whether appliquéing by hand or machine, add all the details to the body before applying the bear to the fabric background. In this way you are handling small pieces of fabric rather than working with the entire quilt fabric.

By hand: Trace each pattern piece for the bear's features and clothing from your enlargements. Transfer each pattern to heavy paper to make a template (see pages x and xiii).

1. Place the template on the correct fabric for each (you will have a seam allowance all around) and draw around the shape.
2. Clip around the seam allowance wherever the fabric curves. Do not clip straight edges. (See page xv for details.) Clip into each corner of the pant bib.
3. Using a medium-hot iron, press the raw edges over the edge of each template all around. Remove the template and press down on the back of the fabric to create a defined crease around the edges.
4. Pin each appliqué in position on the front of the brown body of the bear as indicated in the drawing.
5. Using a slip stitch or straight machine stitch, sew all the elements to the fabric. Press.
6. The black felt buttonholes and eye centers can be glued in place last or machine-stitched around the edge. These pieces are too tiny for turning and, since felt doesn't fray, it is unnecessary to do this.

By machine: The appliqué pieces are cut per the pattern without seam allowance if you are appliquéing with a zigzag stitch.

1. Pin each design element on the brown bear's body in position as indicated on the drawing.
2. Using the thread color of each piece, stitch around all raw edges, but *not* around the outside edges of the bear appliqué.
3. The buttonholes and centers of the eyes can be attached with a tiny zigzag stitch or you can glue them in place.

To assemble

1. Cut a piece of yellow gingham 30$\frac{1}{2}$ × 45 inches ($\frac{1}{4}$-inch seam allowance is included).
2. Cut border strips as follows: 2 strips of brown calico 4$\frac{1}{2}$ × 54$\frac{1}{2}$ inches long and 2 strips 4$\frac{1}{2}$ × 30$\frac{1}{2}$ inches long.
3. With right sides facing and raw edges aligned, stitch the short border strips to the top and bottom of the yellow gingham. Open the seams and press.
4. Repeat with the long side pieces.
5. With right side up, pin the fabric to the quilt batting. Baste around all outside edges to hold in place while quilting.

To quilt

By hand: Clip around all curved edges of bear appliqué in seam allowance. Turn all outside edges of the teddy bear appliqué under $\frac{3}{8}$ inch and press all around.

1. Following the drawing for positioning, pin the bear appliqué to the yellow fabric, catching the batting as well.
2. Using matching thread or 3 strands of matching embroidery floss, take small running stitches or backstitches around the inside edge of the bear shape.
3. Clip and turn the edges of each balloon under and stitch in position in the same way. For more quilting and definition of each appliqué shape you can also stitch along the outer edge of each element on the yellow fabric.

By machine: If you are using a straight rather than zigzag stitch, the edges of the appliqués must still be turned under as for hand quilting. If you use a zigzag stitch, no turning is necessary and your edges will have a decorative finish.

1. Pin the bear in position on the yellow fabric background. Pin each balloon in position.
2. Using a thread color to match each fabric piece, zigzag-stitch around all raw edges.

Each square equals 5″

Fig. 1

3. Machine-sew with a straight stitch along the channels of the border seams. Remove all basting stitches.

To finish

The details on the bear's face below the nose, and the balloon strings are embroidered with a backstitch or running stitch using 3 strands of black floss. If you prefer, they can be applied with waterproof-ink marking pen. The strings can be applied freehand as they do not have to be perfectly straight, or you can use a ruler to draw a light pencil line for each so you have a guide to follow.

To create an accurate mouth, trace the lines for it. Place a piece of carbon paper in position on the fabric with the tracing over the carbon. Retrace over the lines to transfer them to the fabric.

1. Cut brown backing fabric (or another matching fabric) 38$\frac{1}{2}$ × 54$\frac{1}{2}$ inches.
2. With right sides facing and raw edges aligned, pin backing to front and stitch around 3 sides and 4 corners. Clip off each corner piece to seam line.
3. Turn quilt right side out and press. Turn open edges in and stitch closed with a blindstitch.

If you want to catch the backing so it isn't loose, take a few small stitches at each corner of the inside border seams.

PLATE 13   Patchwork Christmas Stocking

PLATE 14   Holiday Centerpiece, Christmas Ornaments

PLATE 15   Patchwork Country Holiday Table Runner

PLATE 16   Pine Tree Wallhanging and Placemat

PLATE 17   Holiday Lone
Star Tablecloth and Seat
Cushions

Courtesy Family Circle
magazine

PLATE 18   Noel Table Decoration

Book Three

First Steps in Quilting for the Holiday Season

PATCHWORK CHRISTMAS STOCKING

Get out your most colorful scraps of fabric. Bright yellows, greens, reds, and blues will make the most cheerful, holiday stocking. For a really elegant decoration, use velvet, satin, silk, and brocade. Because you are using small scraps, you may have a variety of material left over from other projects. Sometimes fabric stores sell bags of scrap pieces, making it easy to put together a nice assortment of colors and textures in one project.

The technique for making this stocking is similar to that used for crazy quilts. There are no individual pattern pieces to trace and enlarge, no seams to match. You simply stitch together fabric scraps and then only enlarge the stocking pattern to cut out the shape.

Materials

2 pieces solid fabric 10 × 15 inches for lining
1 piece of fabric 10 × 15 inches for backing
scraps of colorful calico prints
quilt batting
thread to match fabric colors
tracing paper
heavy paper for template

Directions

You can make the patchwork fabric in one of two ways. If you want to copy the stocking shown here, enlarge the pattern and transfer each piece to cardboard to make a template (see page xiii). Or you can simply stitch together a variety of sizes and shapes of scraps to create a piece of fabric approximately 10 × 15 inches. If you use the pattern pieces provided here, add a 1/4-inch seam allowance to each when cutting out.

1. Refer to the piecing Fig. 1. With right sides facing, join piece 2 to 3. Open seams and press. Join piece 1 to piece 2–3.
2. Next join piece 4 to 5. Open seams and press.
3. Join 6 to 7 in the same way.
4. Join 8 and 9, followed by 10.
5. Join 11 and 12, followed by 13.
6. Join piece 8–9–10 to piece 11–12–13.
7. With right sides facing and raw edges aligned, join all 4 sections in the same way. Open seams and press.
8. Enlarge the stocking pattern (see page xiii) and pin to the backing piece. Cut out leaving a 1/4-inch seam allowance. Cut 2 more stocking pieces from the solid lining fabric without seam allowance.
9. If you have simply stitched several odd pieces of fabric together to create a

patchwork piece, rather than using the pattern pieces provided, use the stocking pattern to cut this shape from your patchwork.

To quilt

1. Cut a stocking shape from the quilt batting, without a seam allowance.
2. Pin the batting to back of the patchwork stocking piece.

3. Using the thread to match each fabric color background, machine- or hand-stitch 1/8 inch inside each seam line. If machine quilting, set stitch length for a slightly longer stitch than that for regular sewing.

To finish

1. With right sides facing and raw edges aligned, pin the backing piece to the quilted top piece and stitch around with a 1/4-inch seam allowance, leaving top edge open. Clip around curved edges to seam line.
2. Turn right side out and press.
3. With right sides facing and raw edges aligned, stitch lining pieces together with a 1/4-inch seam allowance, leaving the top edge open. The lining will be slightly smaller than the stocking. Do not turn right side out.
4. Slip lining into stocking and push toe down in place all around.
5. Fold top edges of stocking and lining to the inside between both layers of fabric and press. Slip-stitch all around top edge. Tack lining and stocking together at the toe and heel in the seam if needed.

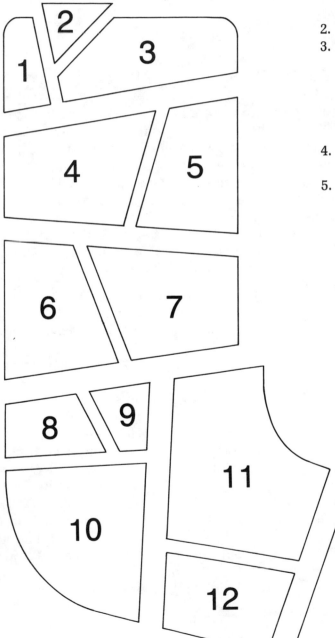

Fig. 1 Patchwork stocking piecing diagram.

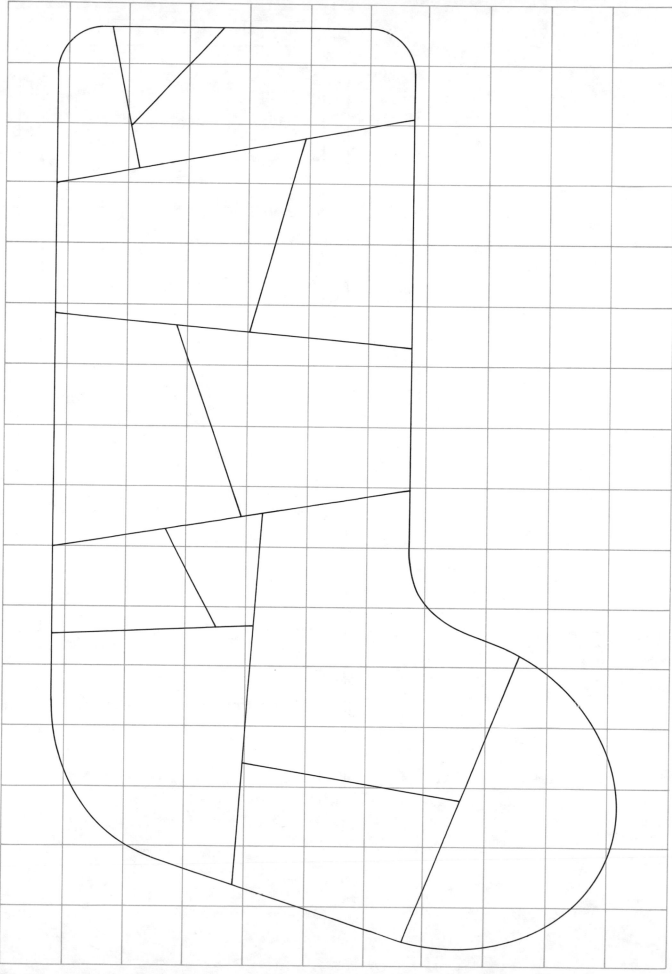

Each square equals 1″   *Fig. 2*

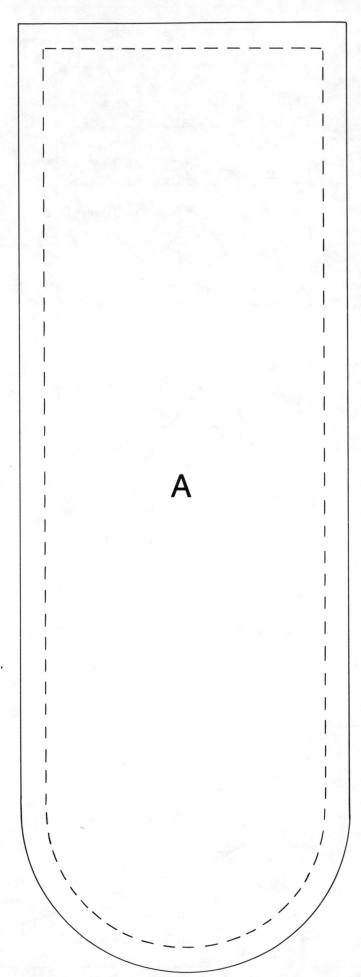

Fig. 1   Holiday centerpiece pattern.

HOLIDAY CENTERPIECE

Make a quilted, petal-shaped cover to fit any flowerpot. This one is 8 inches in diameter and 6½ inches high. Made of 3 different calico prints in red, white, and green, it is a cheerful table decoration. There is only 1 pattern piece and, since the cover is made from stitching each section together, you can add or subtract the number needed to fit your planter.

Materials

¼ yard red calico fabric
¼ yard green calico fabric
¼ yard white calico fabric
⅓ yard solid green fabric for lining
thin quilt batting
tracing paper
heavy paper for template

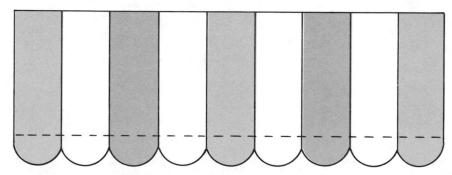

Fig. 2 Christmas centerpiece assembly diagram.

Fig. 3 Finished centerpiece.

Directions

Trace pattern piece A and transfer to heavy paper for template (see page xiii). Use the template (seam allowance included) to draw and cut 3 pieces from each of the calico fabrics.

1. With right sides facing and raw edges aligned, begin at the top of one straight side and stitch a green piece to a white

7

piece for 6 inches only. Open seams and press.

2. Stitch a white piece to the other green edge in the same way. Continue to join pattern pieces, alternating colors. Do not join last 2 edges to form the circle.

3. Place the patchwork fabric piece on the green backing fabric. Pin together on top of batting and cut out green fabric and batting the same as the top.

4. Trim batting piece 1/4 inch all around.

5. With right sides facing, pin fabric pieces to batting piece.

6. Stitch around each curved petal shape to the stitch line of the joining seams. Clip around each curve.

7. Turn right side out and press.

8. With right sides facing together and raw edges aligned, join side edges to form a cylinder. Trim seam and turn right side out.

9. Turn top, raw edges in 1/4 inch and press. Slip-stitch around top edge.

To quilt

Machine-stitch along all seam lines and across each petal 6 inches down from the top edge. You will have a loose petal of each color approximately 2 1/2 inches long. These will turn up and sit on your table top all around the plant.

If you want to do more quilting, draw a grid across the fabric and quilt along marked lines.

CHRISTMAS ORNAMENTS

Make a batch of ornaments from all your colorful fabric scraps. These are traditional patchwork patterns most commonly found in old quilts. The pattern pieces are small and the finished size of each is 4 × 4 inches. This is a good way to practice making templates and sewing patches together. Once you see how easy it is, you'll be ready to use the same patterns and techniques for a larger project, such as a place mat, tablecloth, and finally a quilt or wall hanging.

Materials (for 3 ornaments)

Fabric scraps of dark and light prints with green and red predominating

Polyester stuffing
1½ yards pregathered 1-inch-wide eyelet
12 inches red or green ½-inch-wide satin ribbon
thread to match fabric colors
tracing paper
heavy paper for template

Directions

Trace the triangle pattern piece as shown. The seam allowance is included. Transfer the pattern to heavy paper to make a template (see page xiii). Cut the following pieces of fabric:

(A) Cut 4 light pieces
(A) Cut 4 dark pieces
(B) Cut 8 light pieces
(B) Cut 8 dark pieces

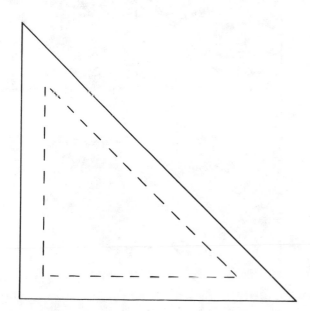
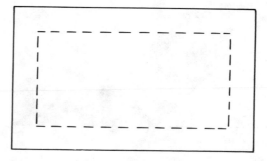

Fig. 1   Christmas ornaments patterns.

Cut 1 piece of backing 4½ × 4½ inches for each ornament.

To assemble

1. Refer to diagram 1. With right sides facing and raw edges aligned, join a light A piece to a dark A piece, leaving a ¼-inch seam allowance. Press seams to the dark side (rather than open) so the fabric doesn't show through the white background.
2. Repeat 3 more times so you have 4 squares 2 × 2 inches.
3. With right sides facing and edges aligned, stitch the 4 squares together to make a 4-inch square. Press seams as before.
4. Refer to diagram 2. With right sides facing and raw edges aligned, stitch a light B to a dark B, leaving a ¼-inch seam allowance. Press seams to the dark side.
5. Repeat 3 more times to make 4 squares 2 × 2 inches.
6. With right sides facing and edges aligned, stitch together according to the diagram.
7. Refer to diagram 3. With right sides facing and edges aligned, stitch a dark B to a light B to make a square. Press seams to one side on dark fabric. Make 3 more squares.

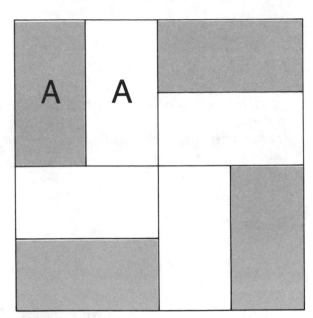

Diagram #1

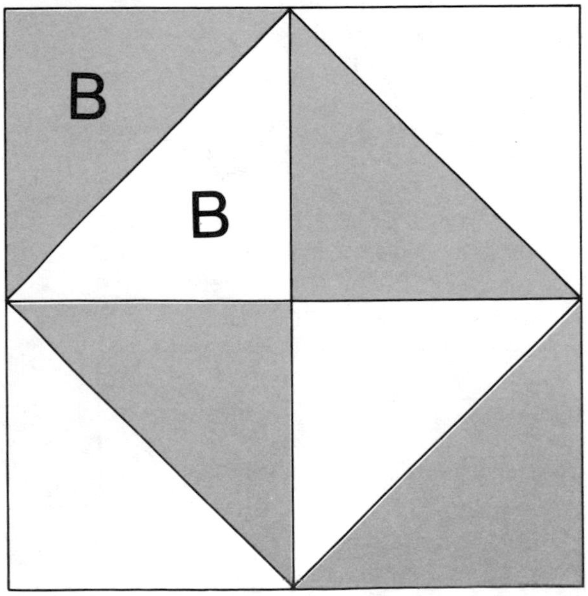

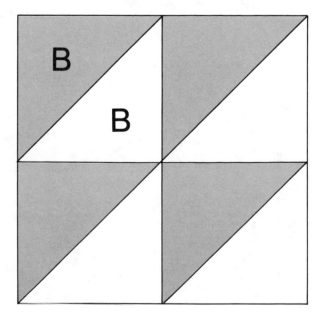

Diagram #2

Diagram #3

Fig. 2   Ornament layouts.

8. Join all 4 squares as shown on diagram.

To make more ornaments, continue to cut out more pattern pieces from a variety of light and dark fabrics. Join each triangle or strip to make the 2-inch squares. Try different ways of assembling the squares to make interesting patterns of the finished 4-inch square. New patterns arc created when you put the squares together in different ways.

To finish

These projects are so small that the patchwork is enough to create a quilt effect. No stitching is required. However, you can add hand or machine stitches 1/8 inch inside each seam.

1. Cut a length of eyelet 16 1/2 inches for each ornament. With right sides facing, stitch the raw ends together to create a loop.
2. With right sides facing and edges aligned, pin the eyelet to the patchwork top all around. Stitch together.
3. Cut a 4-inch length of satin ribbon for each ornament. Fold in half lengthwise and pin the ends together at one corner with the looped end toward the center of the fabric.
4. Place a backing square face down over the ribbon, eyelet, and top fabric piece. Pin at each corner and center of each side.
5. Stitch around 3 sides and 4 corners leaving a 1/4-inch seam allowance. Clip corners off.
6. Turn right side out and press.
7. Stuff with polyester until the ornament is firmly packed. Slip-stitch opening closed and hang.

For a variation, I have used a narrow crocheted lace trim on some of the ornaments. You can also use colorful piping as a trim to replace the eyelet. Attach in the same way.

PATCHWORK TABLE RUNNER

There are 3 different quilting patterns used on this calico runner. All the pattern pieces are triangles, which, when joined, form squares. Each block is a 4-patch pattern. It is important with a project like this to cut your pieces accurately and to sew them all with the same 1/4-inch seam allowance. In this way all your points will meet perfectly, giving you a crisp design. The finished size of the table runner is 16½ × 70½ inches.

Materials

1/4 yard red calico print
1/4 yard tan calico print
1/2 yard white/red/blue calico print
2 yards blue calico print
thin quilt batting
thread to match fabric colors
needle
tracing paper
heavy paper for template

Directions

Trace the 2 pattern pieces, A and B and transfer to heavy paper for template (see page xiii). Use the templates to draw and cut out the following pattern pieces, which include a 1/4-inch seam allowance:

(A) 8 red pieces
(A) 8 tan pieces
(A) 16 white pieces
(B) 4 red pieces
(B) 4 tan pieces
(B) 8 white pieces

Cut 2 blue calico border strips 3½ × 71 inches and 6 strips 3½ × 11 inches.
Cut a blue backing piece 17 × 71 inches.

To make the blocks

There are 5 blocks divided by sashes. There are 3 different patterns of blocks. The first and last blocks are the same. The second and fourth are the same, positioned differently. The middle block is different from both of these.

1. With right sides facing and raw edges aligned, join a red A piece with a white A piece along the long edge (see Fig. 2, block 1). Open seams and press. Repeat.
2. With right sides facing and long, raw edges aligned, join a tan A piece with a white A piece. Open seams and press. Repeat.
3. Join all the squares as shown in diagram. Open seams and press.
4. Follow steps 1 through 3 for second identical block.
5. As above, join a white A piece with a red A piece. Join a white A piece with a tan A piece.
6. Follow Fig. 2, block 2 to join squares, alternating colors in each section.

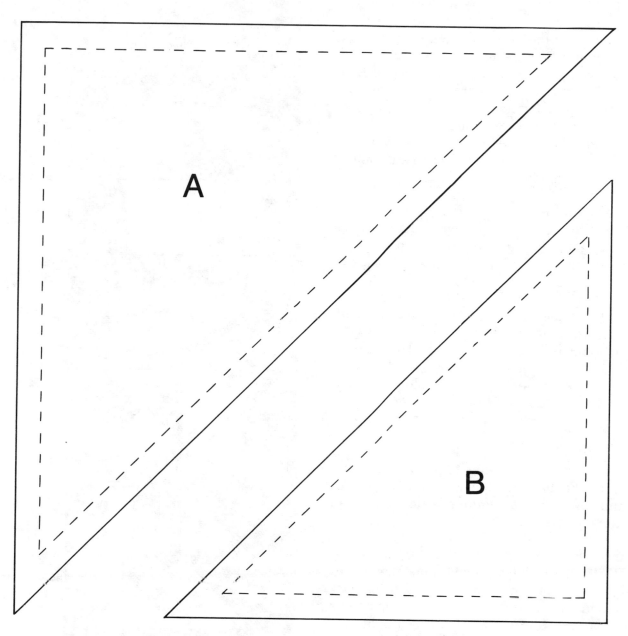

Fig. 1   Patchwork table runner patterns.

7. With right sides facing and raw edges aligned, stitch a red B piece to a white B piece along one short side. Open seams and press. Repeat.

8. Join the 2 triangles to form a square. Repeat.

9. Follow the above directions and join a white B piece with a tan B piece. Repeat and join the triangles together. Make another square in the same way. See Fig. 2, block 3.

10. Make a block as you did for diagram 2. Put the squares together following Fig. 2, block 4, which reverses the color placement.

To assemble

1. With right sides facing and raw edges aligned, join a short blue strip $3^1/2 \times 11$ inches to the left side edge of block 1. Open seams and press.

2. Repeat on opposite side of block.

3. Continue to join blocks in this way according to the diagram.

4. With right sides facing and raw edges aligned, stitch a long border strip $3^1/2 \times 71$ inches to the long runner. Open seams and press.

5. Repeat on opposite side. Press fabric.

To quilt

Cut a strip of batting 16×70 inches and pin to the back of the fabric. Machine- or hand-sew with a running stitch along all seam channels to quilt.

To finish

With right sides facing and raw edges aligned, stitch backing fabric to patchwork top, leaving 12 inches open at one short end for turning. Clip corners and turn right side out. Press. Machine-stitch $1/8$ inch in from the edge all around the top of the runner.

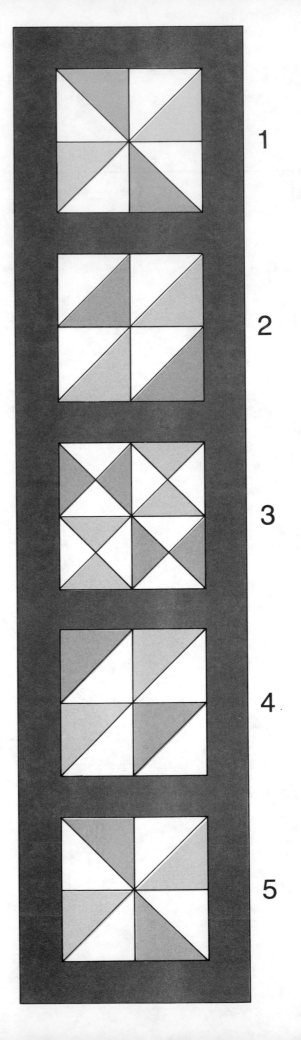

Fig. 2   Patchwork table runner layout.

PINE TREE WALL HANGING

This is a wonderful project to make from a variety of scrap fabric pieces. Create a colorful grove of trees standing against a snow-filled background. The hanging pieced quilt has a country feeling and would be at home in almost any environment. The finished size is 24½ × 26½ inches.

Materials

1 yard white cotton fabric
1 yard dark green print backing material
a variety of colorful fabric scraps
polyester batting
thread to match fabric colors
needle
package of Velcro tabs for hanging

Directions

Trace each pattern piece and transfer to heavy paper for templates (see pages x and xiii). Each template includes a ¼-inch seam allowance. Cut the number of pieces in the following way:

BORDER: Cut the border strips first to be sure you will have long continuous pieces before cutting up the rest of the fabric. From the white fabric cut 2 strips 2 × 22 inches and 2 strips 2 × 26½ inches.

PATTERN A: Cut 2 pieces each for 13 trees from the fabric scraps. Each set can be different or some fabrics can be repeated if desired. You will have 26 triangles all together.

PATTERN B: Cut 52 pieces from white cotton fabric.

PATTERN C: Cut 26 pieces from white fabric.

PATTERN D: Cut 13 tree trunks from dark green printed fabric.

PATTERN E: Cut 8 pieces from white fabric.

PATTERN F: Cut 4 pieces from white fabric.

To make one block

1. With right sides facing and edges aligned, stitch one B piece to one A piece, leaving a ¼-inch seam allowance. Press seams to one side.
2. Follow the assembly diagram and attach a B piece to the opposite side of A. Press seams to one side.
3. Follow the first block assembly and join B to A to B, using the same color for the second A piece as you did for the first in step 1.
4. Join C to D to C with a ¼-inch seam allowance. Open seams and press.
5. With right sides facing and edges aligned, join all 3 strips together, leaving a ¼-inch seam allowance. Open seams and press. Make 13 blocks in this way.

Joining blocks

Place all tree blocks in position on your tabletop. Rearrange the colored blocks until you have a pleasing balance and you like the layout. Join the blocks in vertical strips as follows:

1. For the first left, vertical row, with right sides facing, place one E piece over the bottom of a tree block so it covers the

15

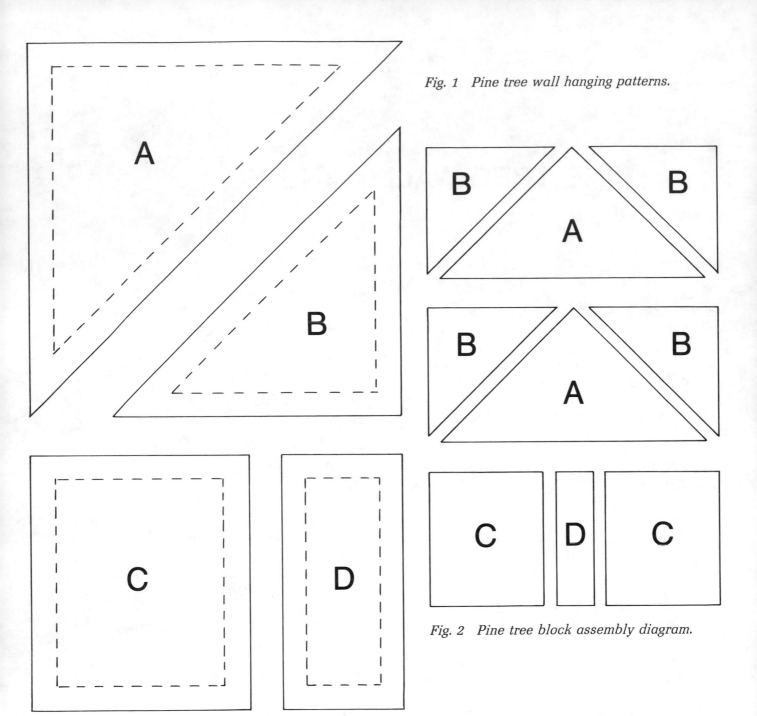

Fig. 1 Pine tree wall hanging patterns.

Fig. 2 Pine tree block assembly diagram.

trunk and the bottom raw edges are aligned. Stitch together with a 1/4-inch seam allowance. Open and press.

2. With right sides facing, join with the next tree block under the first. Open and press seam.

3. Join pattern piece E as before, followed by the last tree block in the first row (see assembly diagram).

4. To create the second row of the wall hanging, place pattern piece F face down on a tree block with top raw edges aligned. Stitch together with a 1/4-inch seam allowance. Open and press seam.

5. Place E piece face down over bottom edge of tree block with edges aligned and stitch together. Continue to join pattern pieces to create alternate rows of pieced fabric.

6. When all 5 rows are complete, join together in the following way: With right sides facing and long edges aligned, join row 1 with row 2, leaving a 1/4-inch seam allowance. Open and press. Join row 3 to row 2 and continue in this way.

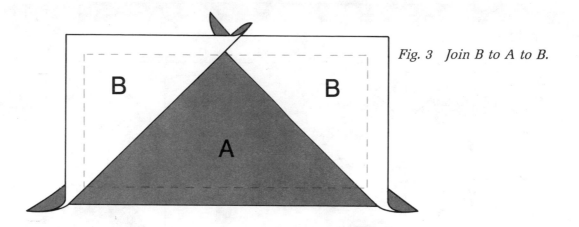

Fig. 3 Join B to A to B.

Making the border

The white border is 1 inch wide and the narrow dark green border is created from the backing as a 1/2-inch finished edge all around.

1. With right sides facing and edges aligned, stitch one 2 × 22-inch strip to the top of the quilt front, leaving 1/4-inch seam allowance.
2. Repeat on the bottom edge. Open seams and press.
3. Join the long, side, border strips 2 × 26 1/2 inches in the same way.

Quilting

The quilting on this wall hanging is easy to do on the machine or by hand. Either way will be effective.

1. Find the center of the top of each E piece. Using a ruler and light pencil or water-soluble pen (once the quilting is complete the pen marks can be easily removed by simply using a plant mister), draw a light diagonal line from this point to each outer corner to create the tree shape.
2. Draw a light line dividing each F piece in half horizontally. Draw the triangle tree shape in each section as you did for pattern piece E.
3. Cut the batting to the same size as the top piece (including white borders).
4. Begin at the center of the quilt front and baste the fabric and batting together with long, loose stitches outward, creating a sunburst pattern. These stitches will be cut away as you do your quilting.
5. *To machine-quilt:* Stitch along all seam channels. Do the same along the

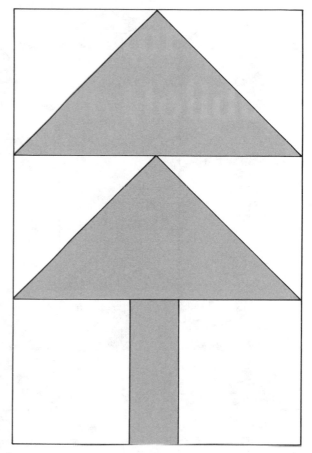

Fig. 4 Completed pine tree block.

predrawn quilt lines on pattern pieces E and F.

To quilt by hand: Use a quilting needle and take small stitches on either side of the seams through the fabric and batting. Do not pull too tightly. (See page xviii for more quilting details.)

To finish

Cut the backing material 1 inch larger than the quilted top piece. Pin the quilted top to

17

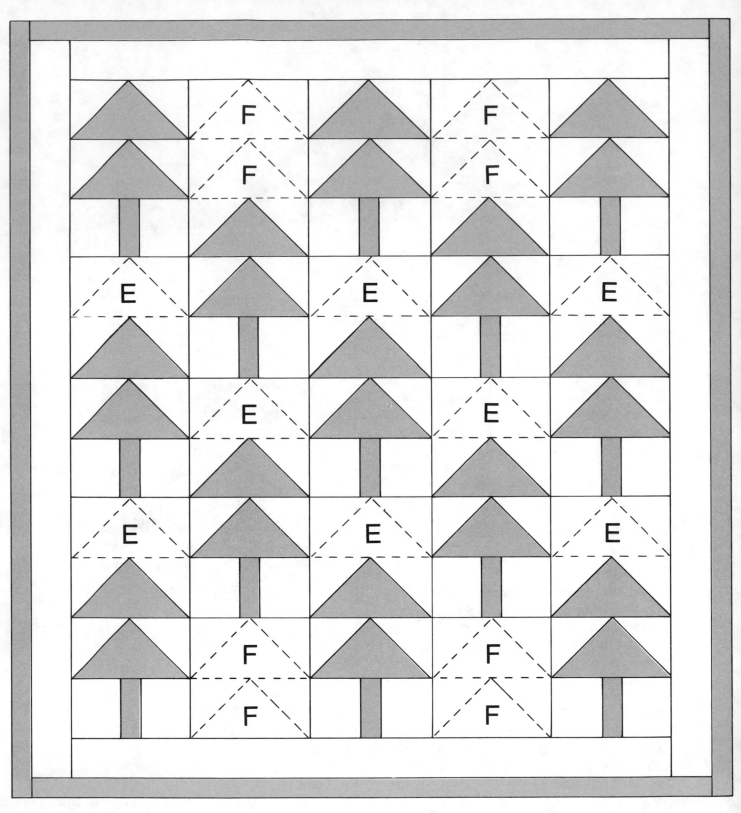

Fig. 5   Pine tree wall hanging diagram.

the backing material with wrong sides facing. Turn the raw edge of the backing forward 1/4 inch and press. Fold over to the front of the top and blindstitch. There will be a 1/2-inch green border all around the quilted wall hanging.

Hanging

Attach a Velcro tab to the back of each corner of the finished project. Attach corresponding tabs to the wall where you will hang the quilt.

PINE TREE PLACE MAT

Make a set of place mats to match the pine tree wall hanging to create a country dining area. The finished size of this simple patchwork project is 12 × 16½ inches. One yard of 45-inch-wide fabric will yield 6 place mats. You can use scraps of fabric for the trees on a snowy white background. For an added touch, appliqué a pine tree on one corner of a napkin.

Materials

1/2 yard dark blue calico
1/2 yard white cotton fabric
small amounts of colorful fabric scraps
dark green fabric scraps for tree trunks
polyester batting
white thread
needle
tracing paper
heavy paper for template

Directions

Trace the pattern pieces and transfer to heavy paper for templates (see pages xi and xiii). Each template includes a 1/4-inch seam allowance. Cut the pattern pieces in the following way:

BORDERS: The border strips should be cut first so that you have long continuous pieces before cutting the patch pieces. Cut 2 strips of white fabric 1 × 15½ inches and 2 strips

1 × 12 inches. Cut one 2 × 15½-inch strip from white fabric for centerpiece F.

PATTERN A: Cut 4 each of 3 different fabric prints.
PATTERN B: Cut 24 from white fabric.
PATTERN C: Cut 12 from white fabric.
PATTERN D: Cut 6 from dark green fabric scraps.
PATTERN E: Cut 4 from white fabric.

To make one block

1. With right sides facing and edges aligned, stitch one B piece to one A piece leaving a 1/4-inch seam allowance. Press seams to one side.
2. Follow the assembly diagram and attach a B piece to the opposite side of A. Press seams to one side.
3. Repeat steps 1 and 2 for the next group of B-A-B sequence. Make 5 more blocks in this way.

Joining blocks

Arrange the tree blocks so that you have two horizontal rows that match in color sequence.

1. With right sides facing, place one E piece over the first tree block and stitch together along the right side edge, leaving a 1/4-inch seam allowance. Open and press seams.
2. Place the next tree block over the first E piece and join as before. Open and press seams. Continue in this way with the next E piece and last tree block in the

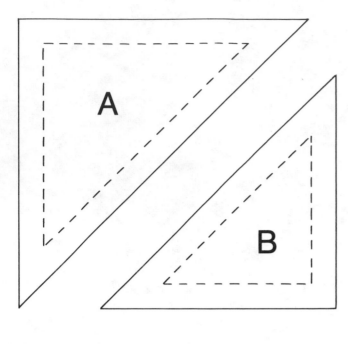

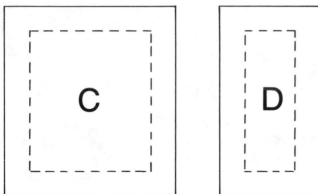

Fig. 1 Pine tree place mat patterns.

from the backing as a 1/4-inch finished edge all around. This dark strip adds definition to the design.

1. With right sides facing and edges aligned, join one 1 × 16-inch strip to the top of the place mat front, leaving a 1/4-inch seam allowance. Open and press.
2. Repeat on the bottom edge.
3. Join the long, side border strips 1 × 12 inches in the same way.

Quilting

You can quilt this as you did the wall hanging, either by machine or hand stitching. Since it is a smaller project, however, you may want to quilt it by hand. This makes it an easy carry-along project or one to work on while watching TV or visiting friends.

row. Repeat to create the bottom row of blocks.

3. Join the rows in the following way: With right sides facing and bottom raw edges aligned, stitch the F strip to the top row of blocks leaving a 1/4-inch seam allowance. Open and press seam.

   With right sides facing and raw edges aligned, join the bottom row of blocks to the F strip, leaving a 1/4-inch seam allowance. Open and press.

Making the border

The white border is 1/2 inch wide and the narrow dark blue calico border is created

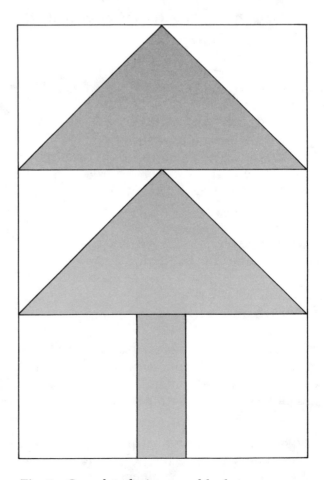

Fig. 2 Completed pine tree block.

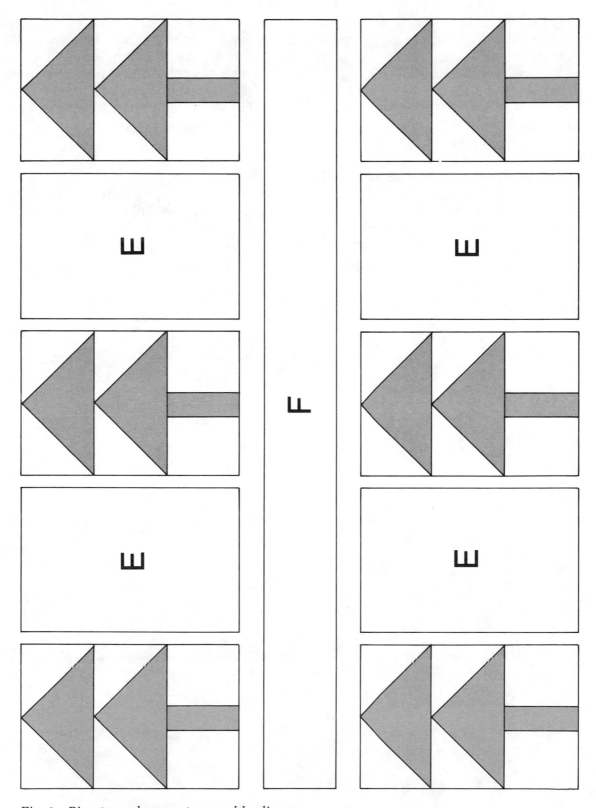

Fig. 3   Pine tree place mat assembly diagram.

1. Using a ruler and light pencil, draw the 2 tree triangle shapes on each E piece to create the tree shape. These are your quilting lines on the white fabric.
2. Repeat along the F strip to create 5 triangle shapes.
3. Cut the batting to the same size as the place mat top, including the white borders.
4. Cut the backing material 1/2 inch larger than the place mat top. Baste front, batting, and backing together.
5. If you are machine quilting, stitch along all the seam channels and drawn lines. For hand quilting, use a quilting needle and thread color to match each fabric piece. Take small running stitches through all 3 layers, along the inside edge of each printed piece. To quilt the white areas, use white thread and follow the drawn lines. (See page xviii for more quilting details.)

To finish

Turn the raw edge of the backing forward 1/4 inch and press. Fold over to the front of the top of the place mat and blindstitch. There will be a 1/4-inch blue calico border all around the place mat.

LONE STAR TABLECLOTH AND SEAT CUSHIONS

A machine-quilted muslin star adds a striking note to any tablecloth. This is a good way to save a stained or worn cloth. Finish the look with padded chair cushions, each with its own star.

The star is appliquéd to the fabric background and the quilting stitches match the tablecloth color. In this case, the stitching is red to match the red plaid tablecloth. Made for a 42-inch round table, the large star must be enlarged. However, the pattern, as is, will fit on most chair seats.

Materials
(for tablecloth and 2 chair seats)

    tablecloth or enough fabric to fit your
      table
    1 yard 45-inch-wide muslin
    1 yard fabric for seat cushions
    quilt batting
    foam rubber for each seat
    piping to measure around cushions
    thread to match fabric
    tracing paper
    heavy paper for templates
    ruler
    hard pencil

Directions

There are 8 diamond pieces for each star. The chair pieces are 8 inches long and 16 inches across the entire star. The tablecloth star pieces are 21 inches long and 42 inches across the entire star.

Trace the pattern piece A and transfer it on heavy paper for template. This is the size to fit chair seats. For the tablecloth, enlarge the pattern (see page xiii) before tracing and transferring to heavy paper for template.

1. Use the appropriate size template and cut 8 pieces of muslin for each project. Seam allowance of 1/4 inch is included.
2. With right sides facing and raw edges aligned, join 2 diamond shapes along one edge. Open seams and press.
3. Continue until you have 4 pieces joined. Set aside and join 4 more pieces in the same way.
4. With right sides facing and raw edge aligned, join both halves of the star to form an 8-pointed appliqué.
5. Turn the raw edges of each point under 1/4 inch and press. Machine-stitch along folded edge.

To quilt
1. Place the star appliqué on quilt batting and cut around the shape. Trim batting slightly smaller.

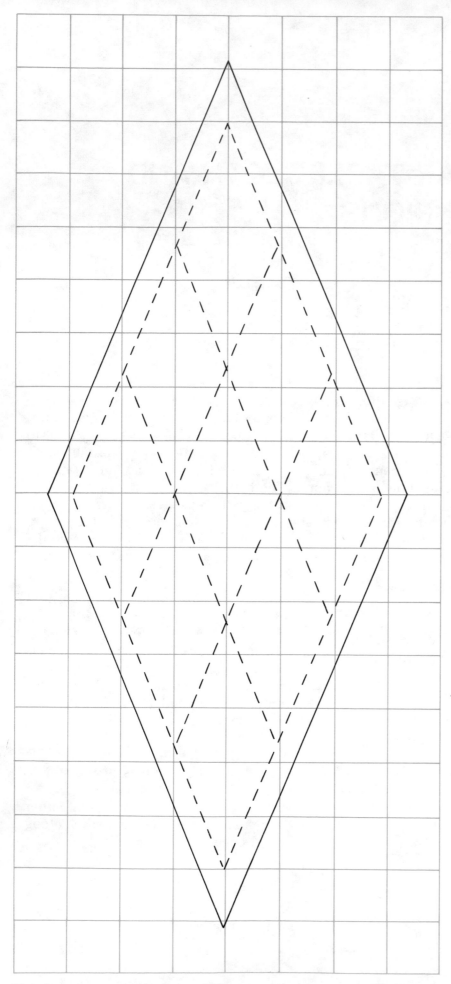

Fig. 1 Lone Star cushion pattern.

Each square equals 1-1/2″

2. Pin batting to wrong side of muslin.
3. Using a ruler and hard pencil, draw a diagonal grid on each section of the star, with approximately 1½ inches between the lines. An easy way to do this is by placing the ruler or yardstick on the fabric, drawing the line, and then flipping the ruler over. In this way you don't have to measure and you are sure of the even spacing.
4. Using a contrasting thread color, stitch along all marked lines to quilt.

To finish

Center the appliqué on the fabric and blindstitch around all outside edges. Tack the center to the fabric underneath. Take a few stitches here and there to secure the appliqué to the fabric. If you have made a very large appliqué you may want to machine-stitch along each seam line between star points.

To finish cushions

1. Make a paper pattern of your seat. You can use a paper bag or any type of paper for this. Use the pattern to cut 2 fabric pieces, adding ¼-inch seam allowance.
2. Attach the appliqué as for the tablecloth. With right sides facing and raw edges aligned, stitch piping around the cushion top piece.

3. Place second piece of fabric right side down over the top piece, piping between, and stitch around, leaving back edge open for turning.
4. Clip around all edges in the seam allowance.
5. Turn right side out and press.
6. Cut a piece of foam rubber (or stuff to desired fullness with Poly-Fil®) and slip-stitch opening closed.

Chair cushion ties

1. Using muslin or appliqué fabric, cut 2 pieces of fabric 1½ × 12½ inches long.
2. Turn raw edges under ¼ inch and press. Turn under another ¼ inch and press. Fold strips in half lengthwise and stitch along edge.
3. Attach the center of each strip to each back corner and tie to chair rails.

Fig. 2 Lone Star assembly diagram.

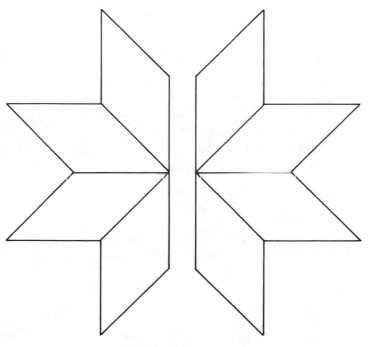

NOEL TABLE DECORATION

At Christmastime it's fun to add holiday cheer to an eating area. A patchwork table-top decoration is the perfect addition. This Noel decoration measures 33 inches across. The border points are made up of the letters spelling N O E L twice in red, white, and green patchwork to contrast with the red center star.

This would make a perfect skirt for a small Christmas tree. If you use a pretty, printed fabric for the backing, you will have a star-shaped table covering to use any time of the year. Simply turn the cloth over after the holidays and use the back side.

Materials

1/4 yard white Christmas calico print
1/2 yard bright green calico
1 yard red calico
1 yard backing material
thin quilt batting
green thread
needle
tracing paper
heavy paper for template

Directions

Trace each pattern piece and transfer to heavy paper or acetate for templates (see page xiii). Each template includes seam al-lowance of 1/4 inch. Cut the fabric in the following way:

(A) 14 green pieces
(B) 8 green pieces
(C) 2 green and 2 white pieces
(D) 4 white pieces
(E) 2 green pieces
(F) 4 white pieces
(G) Place the fold (the broken line) of pattern on fold of fabric and cut so you have a diamond shape. Cut 8 red pieces.

Cut 2 pieces 4 1/2 × 4 1/2 inches from white fabric.

Cut 2 pieces 6 × 6 inches from white fabric.

To make the letters

Refer to piecing diagram for accurate piecing of each letter.

Piecing letter N
1. With right sides facing and edges aligned, sew a white F piece to a green E piece. Open seams and press.
2. Next, join a white F piece to the opposite edge of the green E piece. Open seams and press.
3. Stitch a green B piece to each long edge in the same way. Open seams and press. The letter N is complete. Follow steps 1 through 3 to make another.

Piecing letter O
1. With right sides facing and raw edges aligned, join a green A piece to one side

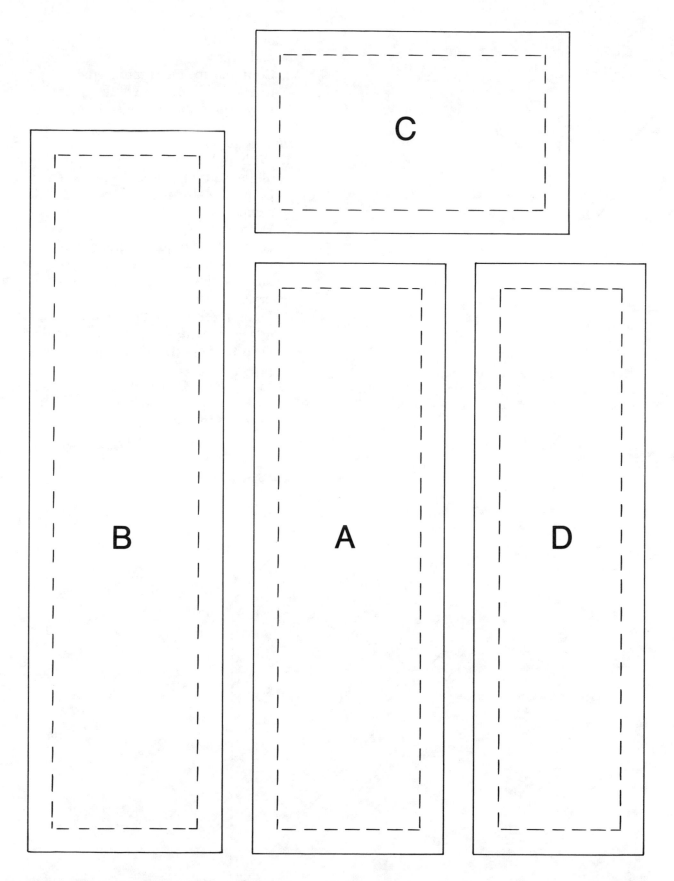

Fig. 1   Noel table decoration patterns.

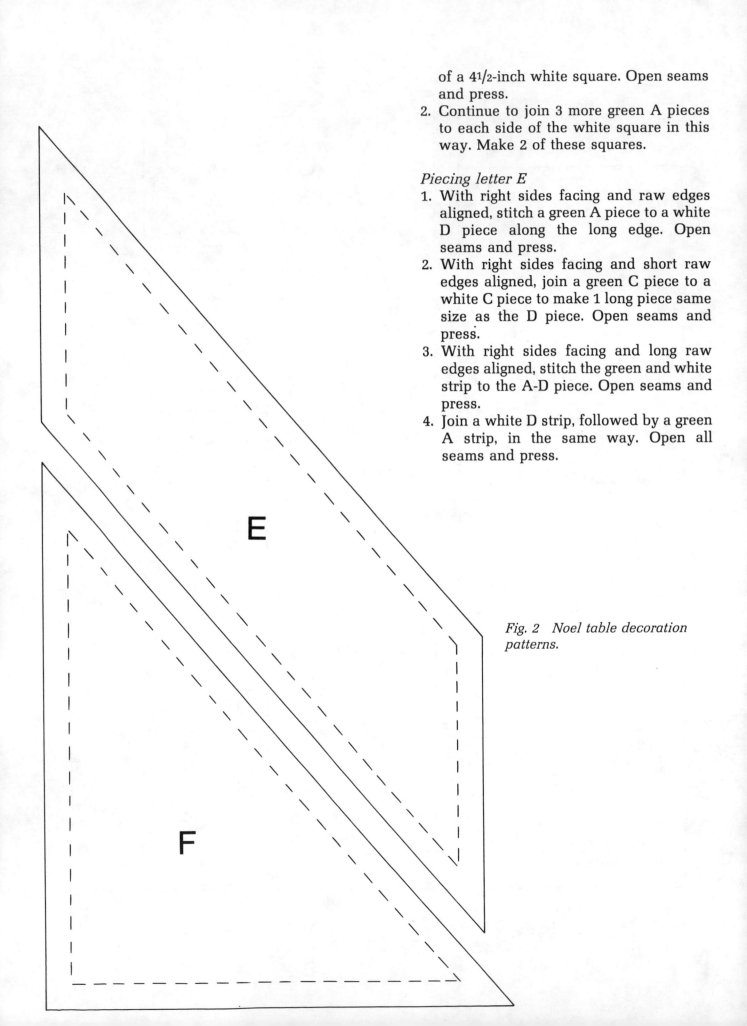

of a 4½-inch white square. Open seams and press.

2. Continue to join 3 more green A pieces to each side of the white square in this way. Make 2 of these squares.

Piecing letter E

1. With right sides facing and raw edges aligned, stitch a green A piece to a white D piece along the long edge. Open seams and press.

2. With right sides facing and short raw edges aligned, join a green C piece to a white C piece to make 1 long piece same size as the D piece. Open seams and press.

3. With right sides facing and long raw edges aligned, stitch the green and white strip to the A-D piece. Open seams and press.

4. Join a white D strip, followed by a green A strip, in the same way. Open all seams and press.

Fig. 2   Noel table decoration patterns.

5. With right sides facing and raw edges aligned, stitch a green B piece to the left side edge as shown in the diagram. Open seams and press. Make 2 of these squares.

Piecing letter L
1. With right sides facing and raw edges aligned, stitch a green A piece to a 6-inch white square. Open seams and press.
2. With right sides facing and raw edges aligned, stitch the long edge of a green B piece to the left edge of the white square and A piece as shown in the diagram. Open seams and press. Make 2 of these squares.

To assemble
Refer to assembly Fig. 4 for piecing the center star and patchwork letters together.

Fig. 3   Noel table decoration patterns.

1. With right sides facing and raw edges aligned, match the point of 2 red G pieces and stitch diamond shapes together as shown. Open seams and press.
2. Repeat 3 times so you have 4 sets of 2 star pieces each.
3. With right sides facing and raw edges aligned, join all 4 sections to complete the 8-pointed star. Trim seams and, if necessary, clip away excess fabric where points come together. Open seams and press.

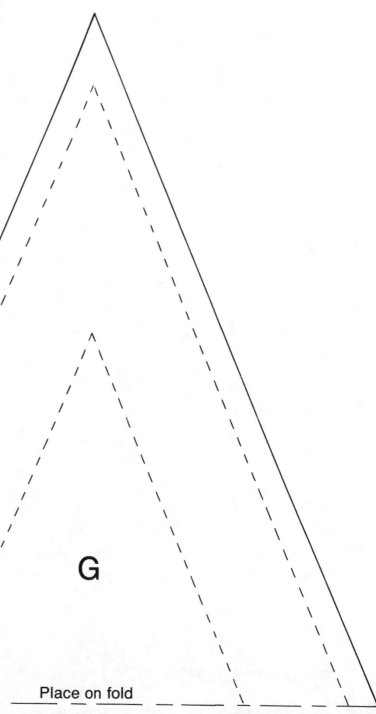

G

Place on fold

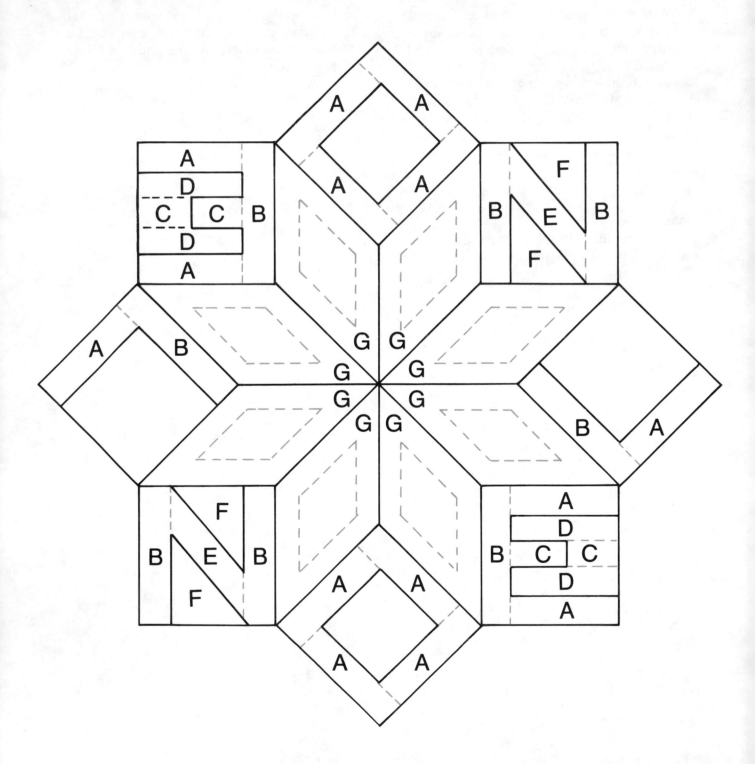

Fig. 4   Noel table decoration piecing diagram.

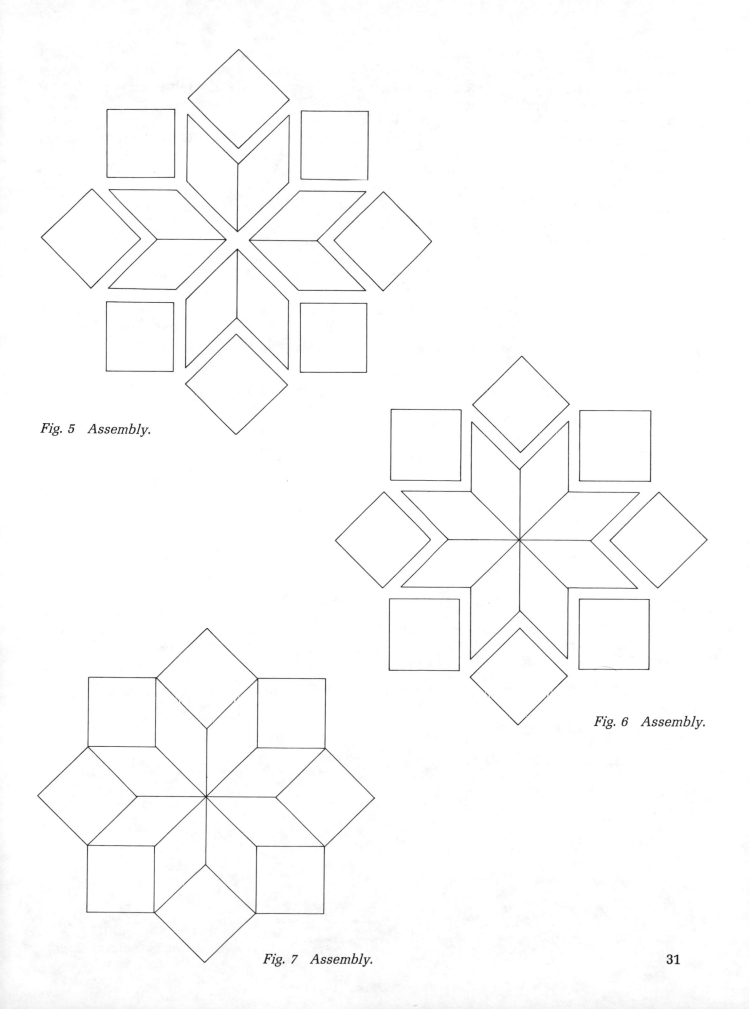

Fig. 5 Assembly.

Fig. 6 Assembly.

Fig. 7 Assembly.

31

4. Refer to Figs. 5 and 6 and join each patchwork letter in the correct sequence. To join each block at the inside point, refer to page xviii for sewing details. This is a tricky area, but it is not difficult to do if you check the diagram that explains this detail.

To quilt

1. Cut out the inside diamond shape from your template of pattern piece G and discard.
2. Place the remaining template on each red diamond shape of the star and draw around the inside cutout area. Repeat on each star piece. These are your quilting lines.
3. Place the entire piece of fabric over the quilt batting and backing fabric and cut out. Trim the batting only slightly smaller than the fabric all around, so it does not extend into the seam allowance.
4. Pin the batting to the back of the top fabric.
5. Using green thread, machine-stitch along the drawn lines. Stitch along all seam lines to quilt.

To finish

With right sides facing and all raw edges and points aligned, stitch top and backing together, leaving 2 adjoining straight edges open for turning. Clip into seam allowance at all points and turn right side out. Press and stitch opening closed with a slip stitch.